Coping with the Uncopable

Learning how to effectively bear the weight of daily problems and pressures in your life

TIMOTHY FLEMMING, SR.

COPING WITH THE UNCOPABLE

Learning how to effectively bear the weight of daily problems and pressures in your life

TIMOTHY FLEMMING, SR.

A Small Independent Publisher with a Big Voice

Printed in the United States of America by
T&J Publishers (Atlanta, GA.)
www.TandJPublishers.com

© Copyright 2016 by Timothy Flemming, Sr.

All rights reserved. This book or parts thereof may not be reproduced in any form, stored in a retrieval system, or transmitted in any form by any means-electronic, mechanical, photocopy, recording, or otherwise-without prior written permission of the publisher, except as provided by United States of America copyright law.

All Bible verses used are from the New King James Version (1982) by Thomas Nelson, Inc., New Life Translation (NLT), and the English Standard Version (ESV)

Cover design by Timothy Flemming, Jr. (T&J Publishers)
Book format and layout by Timothy Flemming, Jr. (T&J Publishers)

ISBN: 978-1-9287522-7-1

To contact author, go to:
www.MCBCATL.org
TFM@mcbcatl.org

DEDICATIONS

First and foremost, I honor and acknowledge my Heavenly Father. Without Your anointing there would be no book to write, no thoughts to share, and no words would have meaning. Thank you for choosing and using me to minister to your people!

To my beloved wife, Virginia, who has stood by me throughout my ministry, I love and appreciate you for all that you do for me and the ministry.

To my sons, Kenneth and Timothy, Jr., thank you for sharing your father for sake of the Ministry.

To my grandchildren, Aric, Timothy, III, Timera, and Jeremiah, you all bring joy to my heart.

To the memory of my son, Aric, who shared in the ministry with me, I know I will see you again one day.

To the Mt. Carmel Baptist Church family, which has supported me over the past thirty years, thank you.

"God is our refuge and strength, a very present help in trouble."—Psalm 46:1

TABLE OF CONTENTS

INTRODUCTION	11
CHAPTER 1: How to Cope with Anger	13
CHAPTER 2: How to Cope with Bitterness	25
CHAPTER 3: How to Cope with Criticism	35
CHAPTER 4: How to Cope with Death	43
CHAPTER 5: How to Cope with Depression	49
CHAPTER 6: How to Cope with Disappointment	59
CHAPTER 7 How to Cope with Fear	67
CHAPTER 8: How to Cope with Hurt	75
CHAPTER 9: How to Cope with Insecurity	83
CHAPTER 10: How to Cope with Loneliness	93
CHAPTER 11: How to Cope with Opposition	101
CHAPTER 12: How to Cope with Rejection	107
CHAPTER 13: How to Cope with Stress	115

Chapter 14: How to Cope with Worry

INTRODUCTION

A significant number of people in today's society are being led and controlled by their emotions. Many of their choices and actions are purely emotionally based. As Christians, we should not rely on our emotions, "For as many as are led by the Spirit of God, they are the sons of God" (Romans 8:14). Therefore, in order to be recognized as true sons and daughters of God, we must be led by the Spirit and not by our emotions.

It is difficult to make the transition from living an emotionally led life to living a spiritually led life. The change from one way of living to another does not come overnight. It is a process that must be studied, practiced, and implemented in our lives. Through practice we learn to manage our emotions. When we successfully manage our emotions, we'll be able to hear the Spirit of God more clearly, and therefore, follow more closely the plan and the path which God has set before us.

Coping with the Uncopable

In this book, I address the most basic human emotions we feel and reveals to us how they are leading our lives on a everyday basis. Each chapter deals with one specific emotion, its causes, and methods for managing it. It includes both biblical references and practical applications which serve as illustrations. The information included in the text will certainly provide you with some of the essential tools for managing your emotions so you can learn to cope with the uncopable.

CHAPTER 1: HOW TO COPE WITH ANGER

"Wherefore putting away lying, speak every man truth with his neighbor: for we are members one of another. Be ye angry and sin not: let not the sun go down upon your wrath: Neither give place to the devil." (Ephesians 4:25-27)

At some point in our lives, we have all gotten angry at something or someone; even God, Himself, has gotten angry with man. In the famous sermon *Sinners in the Hands of an Angry God*, Jonathan Edwards described God's anger towards man by comparing man to a spider hanging from a single thread over a raging fire that's ready to completely engulf it. The fire in this sermon represents the wrath of God. In another analogy, Edwards compares God's wrath to a bow-and-arrow: the bow is pulled to capacity with the arrow aimed directly at the heart of man, ready to be released at any moment; the only thing keeping the arrow from destroying man is God's grace.

There are several examples of God getting angry in the Bible. In the Old Testament, God got angry with His people, the Israelites, after they turned their backs on Him and began to worship idol gods. 1 Kings 11:9-10 says, "And the LORD was angry with Solomon, because his heart was turned from the LORD God of Israel, which had appeared unto him twice, and had commanded him concerning this thing, that he should not go after other gods: but he kept not that which the LORD commanded." Jesus demonstrated great anger towards the religious leaders of His day who were using religion for financial gain—according to John 2:13-15, Jesus physically assaulted the moneychangers in the Jewish Temple with cords and tossed their tables over. Also, in Mark 3:5, Jesus looked upon the Pharisees "with anger, being grieved for the hardness of their hearts" due to their unwillingness to show compassion for a man who was in dire need of a miracle. God gets angry...and so do we. Anger is not a sin, but a natural emotion. It's what you do with your anger that counts.

CAUSES OF ANGER

There are many reasons for God's anger towards mankind. Think about it: God made us and breathed the breath of life into us, and in return, we turn from Him and worship other gods. We allow our money, our cars, our homes, our

Chapter 1: How To Cope With Anger

education, and our gifts to become our gods. God blesses us with good jobs and finances, but we won't pay our tithes to support His church. God blesses us and makes ways for us when we cannot see our way through, but we won't be a blessing to others and help them in their storms.

1. A lack of appreciation

Our lack of appreciation towards God is what causes Him to be angry with us. God's anger towards Christians is justified, but are we justified in our anger towards one another? To know whether or not our anger is justified, we must look at the reasons why we become angry. Once we determine the causes of our anger, we are in a better position to handle it properly.

Anger is often viewed as a negative emotion; and yet, anger has caused some great ideas and events to come forth. Martin Luther was angry when he hung his 95 theses on the Pope's wall and became a leader of the Protestant Reformation. His action enabled people to worship God in their own way. Because a man became angry at watching slaves being beaten and children being snatched from their parents, he made a vow that if he ever acquired power, he would make a change: this man, Abraham Lincoln, became the Present of the United States and he signed the Emancipation Proclamation, the document that ended slavery in America. Because Rosa Parks became angry at having to sit on the back of the bus and decided instead to sit at the front of the bus, the Civil Rights Movement was born, and, today, African Americans have access to places they were restricted from in the past. In the above-mentioned situations, justifiable anger has produced positive changes, but there are times when anger produces negativity.

2. Can't have our own way

Many times, people become angry because they can't have their way. Remember Jonah? Well, according to the first chapter of the book of Jonah, God commanded Jonah to go to Nineveh to preach to the people there. Jonah did not want to go, so he ran from God and boarded a ship to Tarshish, which was in the opposite direction from Ninevah. God caused a storm to arise, which led to Jonah being tossed overboard that ship in into the sea where he was swallowed by a fish. After three days in the belly of the fish, God instructed the fish to release Jonah onto dry land. Afterwards, God commanded Jonah to go to Nineveh once again to deliver His message of repentance. This time, Jonah obeyed; he went into the city proclaiming that God would destroy the city if the people didn't repent. When the people of Ninevah repented, Jonah got angry because he had desperately wanted God to destroy them.

Like Jonah, many of us are determined to have our way. It is natural that when babies come into the world, they cry, kick, and scream in order to get what they want. Many people are alone today because they want everything to go their way, and because they are not willing to compromise, they leave no room for other people in their lives. We have to realize that things won't always go the way that we would like for them to go. We do not live in this world alone. Everything shouldn't go our way because our way is

Chapter 1: How To Cope With Anger

not always God's way. We need to learn how to accept that things should go according to God's plan, not ours.

3. Losing something valuable

Some people are angry because they have lost something valuable such as a loved one, house, car, or a job. We tend to get mad at God when things like this happens, but we must be reminded that God has the sovereign power to both give and take as He sees fit. Also, in many cases, loss is inevitable; it is a way of life. We should not get too wrapped up into people and things. Our focus should be on God. If we focus on God, we can handle loss without becoming angry. Job lost his children, his servants, and his cattle, but he did not become angry with God. Having lost everything he loved, he was still able to say, "Naked came I out of my mother's womb, and naked shall I return there: the Lord gave, and the Lord has taken away; blessed be the name of the Lord" (Job 1:21). Job realized what we often times ignore or forget: Everything belongs to God.

4. Experiencing rejection

Some people get angry when they have been rejected; they may be angry because they think their parents didn't love them or because someone did not give them the attention they desired. There is no doubt that these type of situations affect us and even drive us to anger, but we should seek to develop an understanding of why the rejection has occurred rather than simply assume we know the reason(s) why. If you encounter rejection, don't let it prevent you from living the rest of your life and doing what God called you to do.

Let us look at the story of Joseph. Joseph's brothers rejected him, but he continued to dream. Even when he was sold into slavery and thrown into prison, he never stopped dreaming. As a matter of fact, his dreams were the tools that brought him out of his unpleasant situation. Because he did not let the rejection from his brothers stop him, Joseph found favor in the sight of the Lord (Genesis 37-41). If he had become angry and gave up after he was rejected, Joseph would have never became a ruler in Egypt. Do not let anger keep you from becoming all that God has called you to be.

5. Feeling threatened

Feeling threatened also causes people to become angry. In 1 Samuel 18, we find that even though Saul was the king of Israel, he felt threatened by David. It deeply bothered King Saul when the women of the city sung songs that claimed that David killed tens of thousands, whereas Saul had only killed thousands. Unlike Saul, we must not feel threatened by our fellow Christians. We should realize that another person's blessings and victories won't interfere with ours. Ours blessings and victories will come at the appointed time. God has already designated the date. There's no need to be upset due to another Christian's date coming before yours. You don't know how long they waited or how much they suffered in order to get to where they are.

6. Feeling inadequate

Many people are angry because they wish they could be

Chapter 1: How To Cope With Anger

someone else. Many people don't like who they are. It might shock you to know how many people are depressed because they do not love themselves. Many times, this depression is manifested in the form of anger. Because many are not pleased with themselves, they find it difficult to be pleased with anything or anyone else; they can get a new house, a new car, a new wife or a new husband, but they're still angry. The things that make most people happy do not make angry people happy because their dissatisfaction is deeply rooted within. Giving angry people things does not make them happy. In order for them to be happy, they must first get free within by learning to love and accept who God made them.

Many people don't realize that anger is sometimes a sign of depression. Depression must be faced before it can be overcome. We must discover what it is about ourselves that causes us to feel depressed. Is it our looks? Our weight? Our education? Our finances? Until we discover what is causing this depression, we won't be able to defeat it. But, instead of seeking out the source of the depression, we tend to direct our anger towards those around us because we know that they care about us. If others can care about us, there is no reason that we should not care about ourselves! When we become so discouraged that we find ourselves in a state of depression, we must do as David did in 1 Samuel 30:6: "And David was greatly distressed; for the people spoke of stoning him because the soul of all the people was grieved, every man for his sons and for his daughters; but David encouraged himself in the Lord his God."

7. Wounded pride

Wounded pride is something else that causes anger to manifest. In the fifth chapter of II Kings, we find that Naamon, a high-ranking military official, had a problem with pride. Naamon, who was suffering with leprosy, went to the prophet of God to be healed. Without directly speaking to Naamon, the prophet sent word through his servant to instruct Naamon to wash in the Jordan River seven times. Naamon was offended that the prophet did not come out to meet him face to face, and he was more offended that he instructed him to go and wash in the dirty waters of the Jordan River. Naamon was more concerned about the look of the water than he was the healing power in it. We shouldn't be like Naamon and focus solely on the way things look. Everything will not be so obvious from the outer appearance. Sometimes, your healing will come in muddy waters. When Naamon let go of his pride and washed in the muddy waters, he was healed. Often times, it takes the muddy waters of trouble to cause us to put aside our pride, open our eyes, make us pray, and make us praise God. Do not let wounded pride get you in trouble. When you lay your pride aside, you place yourself in a position to receive blessings from the Lord.

8. Envy

Another cause of anger is envy. In Genesis 4, Cain killed Abel because he was angered by the fact that God respected Abel's offering and not his own. Cain was trying to compete with Abel just like many Christians today try and compete with other Christians. Many of us only want to buy something after someone else buys it. When we can't keep up with what others are doing, we get angry. A lot of ministers are angry with other ministers that have larger churches and congregations or have gifts that they themselves do not possess. As Christians, we have to recognize that everyone will not have the same gift. We must learn to bloom where God has planted us. The size of your church does not determine its effectiveness. So, don't be so concerned about another Christian's gift; instead, focus on stirring up the gift that God has placed inside of you.

OVERCOMING ANGER

Now that we have discussed some of the reasons why people become angry, we can address how to overcome anger. Knowing how to overcome anger is crucial. In Ephesians 4:26, Christians are given permission to be angry; they are not, however, given permission to remain in that state for a prolong period of time. We are instructed to dispose of anger within a certain window of time. We also need to know how to control our anger because uncontrolled anger can develop into more serious issues.

The first way to overcome anger is to recognize the source of it. We must know what causes the anger before we can deal with it. Much of the anger that people experience stems from relationships within their families. Many children are angry because their parents are not married or are divorced. Some children become even angrier when a stepparent comes into their lives. Parents must recognize and deal with these issues early on so that their children do not carry these unresolved issues into their adult lives like so many people have already done. There are many adults who are sill angry with their parents. Many times, this anger is reflected in their treatment of their spouses when their spouse's actions remind them of a parent in one way or another. When the things people do keeps reminding you of something or someone, you haven't gotten over that event or that person from your past. Family relationships are, by no means, the only source of anger; they are, however, underlying factors in many instances where anger is involved. When the source of anger is recognized, these issues can be addressed directly. This recognition will also eliminate problems that surface in other areas because of misdirected anger.

How do you deal with unresolved anger that arises from problematic family relationships? You must first realize that no one is perfect; and secondly, you must take the heartbreak and feelings of anger that you feel to the throne of God and confess it. Anger can easily lead us down a dark road if we bottle it up and neglect to confess it and deal with the emotion (of anger) properly. That is why the Bible tells us to cast our cares at the feet of Jesus in 1 Peter 5:7, knowing that God cares about us. God cares about our emotional state. He sees the things that make us angry and desires to heal our hearts. God doesn't look at our anger and then say, "Hey, just get over it and move on!" No! He knows the difficulty of moving on when angry. That's why gives us the permission to be angry, but urges us to bring the emotion (of anger) to Him so that He can lead and guide us in what to do with it according to Ephesians

Chapter 1: How To Cope With Anger

4:26. When you give God your anger, He will give you His wisdom and understanding. One of the first things God reminds us of is this: We can't expect perfection out of others since we, ourselves, aren't perfect. It's in light of this that we're able to forgive others for their mistakes and shortcomings, knowing that we have plenty of them ourselves.

We must not only bring our anger to God and confess it, but we must also become mindful of how to handle situations where anger is involved. For one, we must learn how to de-escalate situations by using a calm voice. The Bible says, "A soft answer turneth away wrath: but grievous words stir up anger" (Proverbs 15:1). We should always use a calm voice because the way we speak influences people. We have to also be careful about what we say. There are many ways to say the same thing. Choose the way that is most peaceful. Proverbs 16:24 says, "Pleasant words are as an honeycomb, sweet to the soul, and health to the bones." Rather than lead with a criticism or a negative statement, try leading with a complement or acknowledging what a person has done right—this will oftentimes cause a person to become less defensive and more receptive of your criticism. Remember, we have two ears but only one mouth. We should listen more and talk less. A negative word can enter a person's heart and remain there forever. Even if we later apologize, what we have said cannot be erased. We have to think before we speak, and choose our words carefully. If not, we may regret what we've said later.

The final, and the simplest way to overcome anger, is to choose to seek understanding. The more we understand, the less we allow our emotions to overtake and control us. This is why the Bible tells us to be slow to speak and slow to get offended, but swift to listen in James 1:19. When we choose to listen—I mean, really listen—we put ourselves in a position to receive information about a person, which will provide for us an understanding of that person—why they do what they do, say what they say, think like they think, etc. The more informed we become about a person and the causes behind their actions, the less angry we feel towards them.

    The devil desires that our lives be controlled by anger. He will set up the situations like we discussed earlier which cause us to get angry. Satan's ultimate goal is to destroy us. We give him a difficult time doing his job when we testify to God's goodness. He would rather that we stay angry so we will stop going to church and stop praying. He doesn't want us to be living testimonies, so he will use the spouse, the children, the friends, or anyone else who will affect us. He wants to destroy the best Christians. We must remember, though, to let God fight our battles. If God fights the battles for us, we might experience anger, but we will sin not.

CHAPTER 2: HOW TO COPE WITH BITTERNESS

"Wherefore laying aside all malice, and all guile, and hypocrisies, and envies, and all evil speaking, as newborn babes, desire the sincere milk of the word, that you may grow thereby: If so be you have tasted that the Lord is gracious." (1 Peter 2:1-3).

"Let all bitterness, and wrath, and anger, and clamor and evil speaking, be put away from you, with all malice: And be ye kind one of another, tenderhearted forgiving one another, even as God for Christ's sake hath forgiven you." (Ephesians 4:31-32).

BITTERNESS IS AN EMOTION THAT IS BORN OUT OF anger. When a person is angry for an extended period of time, they ultimately become bitter. A bitter person is not happy; they may have a nice house, a new car, and other nice material possessions, but these things can't turn their bitterness into kindness because houses and cars are external possessions and bitterness is an internal emotion. A bitter person needs internal surgery, which doctors cannot perform. Doctors can perform heart transplants, but they cannot give a person a pure heart.

SIGNS OF BITTERNESS

1. Easily offended

Bitter people are easily offended; they get too sensitive and upset by things that people say; also, they rarely laugh at jokes, and most people find themselves having to apologize to them for the things they have said, even though they did not intend to offend them. Bitter people are also offended by the way people look at them; they quickly assume that people do not like them because of how they look.

2. Closed-off

Many bitter people are quiet and keep to themselves. They find it difficult to laugh and talk because they are uncomfortable with themselves and they aren't free from within; they also hold in their feelings because they don't feel comfortable expressing themselves; and yet, when they are confronted with a conversation or action that triggers their bitterness, they suddenly explode. They are quick to talk about others, but slow to talk about themselves to others.

3. Self-pitying

Bitter people are consumed with self-pity, and they cry of-

Chapter 2: How To Cope With Bitterness

ten just to get other people's attention. They desire sympathy from others; but even when they do receive sympathy, their bitterness is not cured. Bitter people often hurt those who are reaching out to help them and use their bitterness as an excuse to mistreat people those closest to them.

4. Uncooperative

It is difficult to get bitter people to cooperate. I once pastured a church where almost everyone within was bitter. When people are bitter, they hate to see anyone else happy, especially their leaders. It's sad, but bitter church members are never satisfied with their pastor. They always find reasons to complain. If the pastor wears nice clothes and has a nice car, they accuse him or her of stealing money from the church; if, on the other hand, he or she does not dress nice or have a nice car, they accuse him or her of not representing their church well. If his or her sermons are long, they say that the service is too lengthy, but if his sermons are short, they say that he or she did not study and prepare. Bitter people will always find fault with others although they never seem to find fault with themselves.

5. Harboring hurt

All bitter people have experienced some form of hurt; and as a result, they feel as if everyone is out to hurt them; they always remind people of their hurt because they don't know how to get beyond their hurt. When they have been hurt in a relationship, bitter people tend to shy away from new relationships. They are afraid to get close to anyone because they are always expecting to get hurt. Bitter people do not trust many people—if any.

The unfortunate thing about allowing hurt to cause you to distrust people is that you'll find yourself alone and angry because you are alone. Oftentimes, bitter people will complain that no one wants to be around them when, in fact, they are the ones driving everyone away from them—in essence, they are their own worse enemy.

6. Distrust others

Again, as I just mentioned, bitterness will cause us to distrust others due to a bad experience we had with someone else. We isolate ourselves physically and emotionally due to distrust; and in return, we bring even more pain to our hearts because...no one was meant to be alone in life. If we are going to make it in this world and experience any kind of happiness, we must open up and trust someone.

7. Vengeful

Bitter people are revenge-seeking individuals; they seek to destroy anyone who crosses them, and they are usually bitter from past events and they tend to direct their bitterness towards those in their own lives at the present time. There are some women who turn away from their husbands because of bad experiences they have had with their fathers. Most men who rape women are bitter about an experience they had with a woman in the past; their anger usually has nothing to do with the women that they are raping. There are others who mistreat the people they are involved with in relationships because they are bitter about something that happened to them in previous relationships. Bitter

Chapter 2: How To Cope With Bitterness

people are always looking to inflict revenge on someone, and it's usually those closest to them who experience their wrath; they want to strike back at somebody, and in most cases, it is not the person that has caused them to be bitter in the first place; it usually someone else.

8. Overly critical of others

It's been said before: "Misery loves company." Well, bitterness loves company, too. Bitter people often look for bitterness in other people, and if they do not find it, they'll try to provoke it—they feel that if they can provoke bitterness in others, then their bitterness will be justified. If a bitter person curses you and you do not curse them back, they usually feel ashamed and uncomfortable; they are not pleased when they are being mean but you are being kind and pleasant in return. Bitter people need you and I to be bitter just as they are. If you become bitter and curse, then your bitterness becomes their excuse to curse and remain bitter.

9. In denial

It is common for bitter people to deny the fact that they are bitter. When you comment on their actions and their attitudes, bitter people usually claim that what they said or did stemmed from something other than bitterness—they try to convince you of this because they have not accepted the fact that they are bitter, and they do not want your assessment of them to be correct. As a result of this, bitter people find excuses other than bitterness to offer as justifications for their words and actions; they deny the fact that they are unforgiving and desire to hurt others with their actions and words just to make themselves feel better.

10. Angry with God

Bitter people are not just angry with other people, but they are many times angry with God. People become bitter towards God when He doesn't do what they want Him to do or does things they don't want Him to do, or sends them to places they do not want to go. For example, let us look at the prophet Jonah again. Jonah was so angry with the people of Nineveh that the became bitter when God instructed him to go there and preach to the people. Even after he was swallowed by a "prepared fish" and then released and given another opportunity to follow God's instructions, he was still bitter—he obeyed God's instructions with a bitter spirit. After completing his task, Jonah sat down under a tree in the hot sun, moping and complaining about the mercy of God towards the people of Ninevah; and while complaining, God confronted his attitude once again when He removed the shade Jonah was enjoying while in the hot sun. God was teaching Jonah to accept that He is sovereign and can save whomever He chooses and use whomever He chooses. We don't control God.

11. Unhappy

Just like Jonah, many of us don't want to be in the positions God has placed us. Some people are bitter over the husband or the wife God gave them. Some people are bitter over the jobs they have. We often overlook the fact that

Chapter 2: How To Cope With Bitterness

God places us in situations for a reason: He needs for us to do things that no one else can do; He places certain loads on us because He knows that we can handle them. How does God know this? He knows because He created us to handle them. It is no accident that you are a person who everybody depends on. God made you strong because He knew that there were those who would need someone to lean on—someone like you. God has equipped us for each place He sends us to, and He knows what is best. There's no need for us to be bitter. Even when the loads seem too much to bear, we can rest assured that if God placed it on us, He'll help us to carry it. It's not important that we are where we want to be; it's important that we are where God wants us to be; and most importantly, it is important that we learn as the Apostle Paul did to be content in whatever state we are in, knowing that "godliness with contentment is great gain" (1 Timothy 6:6). So, you will never ever truly be happy in life until you get into the place that God wants you to be in.

12. Unmerciful and unforgiving

Jonah didn't want to go to Nineveh to preach repentance because he really wanted God to kill the people of that city. Many of us are bitter because we wanted God to kill certain people as opposed to extend grace and mercy towards them and give them the chance to repent. Many of us are bitter because we want God to kill all our enemies, but He won't. We forget that, at one point, we, too, were enemies of God, but He forgave us and allowed us to live. He loves those we despise just as much as He loves us; after all, they are His creation also (Romans 5:10).

13. Unwilling to change and/or accept changes
Some people are bitter because they do not like new things. Because the practices of Christianity were against his traditional religious practices, Paul persecuted the church (Acts 9). Many of today's Christians become bitter when new things are introduced and implemented in the church—and yes, some changes aren't good and shouldn't be accepted, but some changes are positive and shouldn't be opposed. Some people think things should always go the way they have always gone, but God has said, "Behold, I make all things new" (Revelation 21:5). God is in the business of making changes where they're needed, and we have to be ready and willing to change. Things will not always be the way we want them to be. We have to learn to accept God's way, realizing that we can't control God nor control everyone else; either this or we will become bitter.

HOW TO HANDLE BITTERNESS
When we find ourselves in a state of bitterness, we must be determined to overcome it; and in order to overcome bitterness, we must know who is behind it: Satan. If you are a child of God, bitterness is one of the weapons Satan uses against you. He wants you to be selfish, and therefore, unhappy when life doesn't go the way you want it to go. Satan wants you to focus only on yourself and not God and His will. Satan wants to steal your joy because he knows that the joy of the Lord is your strength (Nehemiah 8:10)—and joy isn't based on what goes on around you, but what

Chapter 2: How To Cope With Bitterness

lies within you. Satan does not want you to rejoice because it strengthens you spiritually, and it allows others to see the goodness of God.

Bitterness can be prevented if we cut it off at the root by not allowing anger to fester too long. Remember: the Bible says to "let not the sun go down upon your wrath" in Ephesians chapter 4. That means we must deal with the negative feelings we have in a timely manner rather than allow them to linger. Confront issues when they first appear. The longer the bitterness sits, and the harder it is to overcome it. If you experience hurts and disappointments which make you angry and lead to bitterness, you should confront the issues by communicating your feelings to those person or persons involved immediately. Tell them how you feel about what they said or did to you and get it off of your chest. Try to understand others. Most importantly, forgive as quick as possible. Forgiveness is not for the other person's sake; it is for your sake: it prevents your heart from become cold and hardened and bitter. Lastly, do not continue to dwell on the things of the past; instead, think about the future that God has for you. As the Apostle Paul declared,

> "Forgetting those things that are behind, and reaching forth unto those things which are before…press toward the mark for the prize of the high calling of God in Jesus Christ" (Philippians 4:13-14).

Coping with the Uncopable

CHAPTER 3: HOW TO COPE WITH CRITICISM

"Blessed are they, which are persecuted for righteousness' sake: for theirs is the kingdom of heaven. Blessed are ye, when men shall revile you, and persecute you, and shall say all manner of evil against you falsely, for my sake. Rejoice, and be exceeding glad: for great is your reward in heaven: for so persecuted they the prophets which were before you." (Matthew 5:10-12)

EVERYONE HAS RECEIVED CRITICISM AT SOME POINT in time. In some cases, we are criticized for the sake of improving in a particular area or situation. This is called constructive criticism. When we understand that the motive of the criticism is constructive, we usually have no difficulty in accepting it; however, when we feel that the criticism is given with negative intentions, we find it difficult to accept. Unfortunately, much of the criticism we receive, especially in the area of our Christian walk, falls into the latter category. It is important, therefore, that we consider the source of such criticism and explore avenues for coping with it.

REASONS PEOPLE CRITICIZE OTHERS
1. Love to gossip
Many people criticize others simply because they love to gossip. The Bible has an interesting term for gossipers in the Old Testament: it calls them *whisperers, slanderers,* and *talebearers*. The Bible has a lot to say about the destructiveness of gossip and the destructive nature of gossipers:

> "The words of a whisperer are like delicious morsels; they go down into the inner parts of the body."—Proverbs 18:8 (ESV)

> "Whoever goes about slandering reveals secrets; therefore do not associate with a simple babbler."—Proverbs 20:19 (ESV)

> "A troublemaker plants seeds of strife; gossip separates the best of friends."—Proverbs 16:28 (NLT)

> "Fire goes out without wood, and quarrels disappear when gossip stops."—Proverbs 26:20 (NLT)

But let's not stop there. The Bible also has something to

Chapter 3: How To Cope With Criticism

say about the nature of those who love to listen to gossip:

> "An evildoer listens to wicked lips, and a liar gives ear to a mischievous tongue."—Proverbs 17:4 (ESV)

> "Interfering in someone else's argument is as foolish as yanking a dog's ears."—Proverbs 26:17 (NLT)

Some people who enjoy gossiping have no intentions of hurting the people they talk about—they're merely making conversation because they are lonely, bored, or depressed. Sadly, however, gossipers rarely seem to realize how much damage their words cause. Talking about the situations of others helps some people divert their attention away from themselves. People who are busy taking care of their needs and the needs of God's people have no time to gossip on others; instead, they will pray for others and then focus on the things God has called them to do. The Bible instructs us in Ephesians 4:29: "Let no corrupting talk come out of your mouths, but only such as is good for building up, as fits the occasion, that it may give grace to those who hear" (ESV). Rather than make sport of someone's problems just so that you can divert attention away from yourself or make yourself feel better, pray for that person and speak that which is edifying to them, that which builds them up and helps them to draw close to God.

People who concern themselves with the affairs of others are prime targets to be used by the devil. The devil uses these people to criticize Christians and prevent them from going forward. Be careful not to let the devil borrow your tongue to destroy another child of God.

Criticism is one of his most powerful weapons. Many Christians can overcome personal issues such as anger and bitterness, but we find it difficult to overcome criticism. We do not like it when people defame our character by slandering us and lying on us, especially when we are simply seeking to please God. If we allow their criticism to discourage us and stop us from moving forward, then the devil will be able to defeat us! His job is to cause us to give up on the things that we believe in and the works that we are doing for God.

The devil used negative criticism in his attempt to stop Jesus from fulfilling His mission on earth. The people constantly ridiculed Jesus and criticized Him for His actions, but Jesus did not allow that to stop Him; He, instead, continued on His journey to the cross. Even while Jesus was hanging on the cross, the people criticized, mocked and scorned Him. Jesus simply withstood the criticism of the people and He completed the task He was destined for: He died the cross for our sins. The Bible says that the servant is no better than their master, so how can we expect not to be criticized as Christians when our Lord and Savior, Jesus, was criticized?

2. Don't believe success is possible
One reason people criticize others is because they do not believe that people have the ability to carry out their plans successfully. When I first mentioned the idea that the Lord gave me for building our church at our present location,

Chapter 3: How To Cope With Criticism

many people did not believe it was possible. Our church had moved three times in the same neighborhood, and many critics simply did not believe we would be able to move from our old neighborhood; they didn't think that we would ever be able to afford to move. Even after we purchased the land to build in a new territory, many still criticized. Once we began to clear the land, there was more criticism, and we were challenged by many within the community, but we did not let criticism stop us; we, instead, continued to move forward; and as a result of this, we were able to complete the construction of our new edifice and move out of the old church and neighborhood. And since that time, we have added a family life center and acquired additional properties around the church to use in our efforts to complete God's plans for our ministry.

THE POSITIVE SIDE OF BEING CRITICIZED

It is Satan's goal to hinder God's people by causing us to stop praying and praising God. The devil uses criticism to stop us because he knows that we prefer to hear compliments. We want people to tell us that we are doing a good job and that they like us. We prefer to be popular, but it is not about popularity; it is about God. One reason God allows criticism is because He wants us to focus our attention in the right direction: rather than focusing on the praise of people, God wants us to focus on His will for us and rely on His power to accomplish His will. Another reason God allows us to be criticized is so that we will know how it feels to be criticized. If we know the pain and confusion that it causes, we will be less likely to criticize others. We will remember the pain that we felt when we were criticized. By allowing others to criticize us, God is able to develop in us the compassion needed to help those who have fallen or are going through rather than criticize them and shame them.

Unfortunately, our biggest critics are often times those whom we love and respect the most: our relatives. This is because they know us better than most people. They know our strengths and weaknesses. Even Jesus' brothers and sisters did not own Him—this is likely contributed to the fact that they grew up together. They found it difficult to accept Him as the Son of God because they had known Him all of their lives as their oldest brother. Joseph, in the Old Testament, was criticized by his brothers as well. They sold him into slavery because God showed him in a dream that he would one day rule over them (Genesis 37). The enemy often uses family members as critics because they are the closet people to us, and their opinions affect us the most. Remember: Jesus said, "A prophet is honored everywhere except in his own hometown and among his relatives and his own family" (Mark 6:4, NLT).

HOW TO DEAL WITH CRITICISM

When we find ourselves being criticized, we should not look at it negatively; but rather, we should realize that if we are being picked out to be picked on, we are special to God. Remember Job? God told Satan that there was none like him in the earth (Job 1:8). God trusted Job and believed that he would not forsake Him. He knew that Job would praise Him despite the situation. So, when you are

Chapter 3: How To Cope With Criticism

being criticized, it is because God trusts you, and you are special to Him. If the devil is not sending criticism your way, it's probably because you're not actively doing God's will. We never criticize the onlookers sitting in the crowd; we only criticize the players who are in the game.

When you are criticized, you can overcome it if you have a desire to succeed despite what others say and think. Do not be hindered by what people say about you or your family. Do not worry about your past mistakes. If you ask God to forgive you, He will. He already has a path laid out for your life. Do not let the criticism of others distract you and cause you to step off course, hindering your journey. God will walk with you as long as you are willing to move forward!

Coping with the Uncopable

CHAPTER 4: HOW TO COPE WITH DEATH

"So when this corruptible shall have put on incorruption, and this mortal shall have put on immortality, then shall be brought to pass the saying that is written, Death is swallowed up in victory. O death where is they sting? O grave, where is thy victory." (1 Corinthians 15:54-55)

MOST PEOPLE DO NOT LIKE TO DISCUSS DEATH. They are interested in going to heaven, but they are not interested in dying. The one thing that frightens people about death is that it is no respecter of persons. Neither our status, our looks, nor our possessions matter to death. Death will overtake the rich as well as the poor, the young as well as the old. There's nothing in life that can keep us from death; it will meet us all at the appointed place and time.

There is a story told about one man who was afraid to die. The man lived in New York City, but when he heard that Death was seeking him he fled to Chicago. One of his friends met Death in New York and asked him if he had an appointment with his friend. Death responded, "Yes." The man then informed Death that his friend was out of town. Death replied, "I know. I was scheduled to meet him in Chicago."

WHY PEOPLE FEAR DEATH

People are afraid of death for several reasons. One reason people are afraid of death is it represents the unknown. We are afraid of things that we do not know much about. We have our own ideas about life after death, but we will never know what it is like until after we die. Another reason people are afraid of death is it separates us from our loved ones. We fear death because it's intrusive. We never know when or where death will appear; it is never invited, it just shows up. People also fear death because it interrupts their plans for the future. The fact that we can't control death intensifies our fear of it. Fortunately, there is someone that has power over death: Jesus Christ.

POWER OVER DEATH

Because God is the only One who has the power of death in His hands, many people become angry with Him when they lose friends and loved ones—they wonder how and why God would allow this. I understand these questions—

Chapter 4: How To Cope With Death

I asked them myself when my 22-year-old son was killed by a drunk driver, but I had to be reminded that dying is a part of living. On the day we are born, we begin our journey towards death. Each day we grow closer and closer to the date of death that has already been assigned to us.

Let us look at the death of Lazarus. The Bible tells us in John 11:5 that Jesus loved Martha and her sister, Mary. Jesus also loved Lazarus, who He considered to be a friend. These were Jesus' friends. One day, Lazarus got sick. It is important to note that knowing Jesus does not exempt us from sickness. Lazarus knew Jesus well; nonetheless, he still got sick. Lazarus was afflicted with physical sickness, but there are other types of sicknesses that affect us. We often experience mental, emotional, and spiritual sickness. But, even in the midst of our sickness, Jesus remains our friend. Our sickness should not determine our relationship with Him. We should love and worship Him in both sickness and health.

Not only did Lazarus get sick, but he died. He was Jesus' friend, but he still died. Mary and Martha were upset about his death, and like most of us, they wondered why God allowed it to happen. A lot of times, people think that God uses death or sickness and pain to punish them. Although we do not like to feel the pain that comes with sickness and death, it can be beneficial to us. A lot of times, these situations cause us to pray and seek God more. They may be tests to see how we respond in times of trouble. We should not ask God to move the pain; we should ask Him to help us bear it, for we know that we cannot do it alone. As we allow God to soothe our pain, our relationship with Him grows stronger. These painful experiences often move us into bigger and better things. We may never get the new job God has for us if we do not accept losing he old. We can never experience a healing if we never get sick. Don't turn away from God during times of sickness and death! Reach out to Him because He knows exactly what your needs are, and He is able to meet them. Your painful experiences are NOT signs that God does not love you; they may mean that He believes in you!

Jesus wept at the grave of Lazarus. This indicates to us that Jesus has compassion for his people. Not only did He weep for Lazarus, but He wept for Martha and Mary as well. Because of His compassion, Jesus spoke life into Lazarus by calling him forth from the grave. Just as Jesus called Lazarus from the grave of death, He has called us from the grave of sin. When we receive salvation, we are given life.

When Jesus promised Martha that she would see her brother, Lazarus, again, she assumed that He was speaking of the Resurrection Day when Christ will return in the last days to set up His earthly kingdom. Jesus corrected her, however, by reminding her that He *is* the Resurrection. Jesus was able to make that statement because He has power over death.

Death is the product of sin. When the world was without sin, there was no need for death. When Adam sinned against God, he became subject to spiritual and physical death. For, God told Adam in the Garden of Eden that the day that he eats from the tree of knowledge of good and evil, he shall surely die—and, by "die",

Chapter 4: How To Cope With Death

God was referring to both a spiritual death and eventually, the physical death. Because, through sin, death was given power over mankind, mankind had to be redeemed from the hands of death. God was able to redeem man's spirit easily because God is a Spirit, but the only way He could redeem mankind physically was by taking on flesh and succumbing to death. As Jesus died on the cross, He said, "It is finished" (John 19:30). He had overcome death by dying Himself only to rise again. Thus, Jesus, through His death on the cross, not only did He provide salvation and redemption for us spiritually, but those who accept salvation through Christ will also receive a new resurrected body one day—yes, we will receive new physical bodies. This is why Paul was able to taunt death by asking, "Death, where is your sting…Grave where is your victory?" This is also why Paul was able to declare, "…to live is Christ, and to die is gain" (Philippians 1:21). Once Jesus conquered death, there was no need for Christians to fear death.

Death destroys the flesh, but it does not destroy the spirit of man, which is his true essence. Believers in Christ may die physically, but they never truly die because Jesus has promised eternal life to those who believe in Him. They simply shed their earthly, mortal bodies for a new, superior body; they simply transition from earth to heaven where no pain and sorrow exists. If we keep this in mind, we will have no fear of death for ourselves or our loved ones. Instead, we will rejoice in the fact that we know Christ, who is the RESURRECTION!

Coping with the Uncopable

CHAPTER 5: HOW TO COPE WITH DEPRESSION

"I will say unto God my rock, why hast thou forgotten me? Why go I mourning because of the oppression of the enemy?" (Psalms 42:9)

"Why art thou cast down, O my soul? And why art thou disquieted within me? Hope thou in God: for I shall yet praise him, who is the health of my Countenance, and my God." (Psalm 42:11)

A T SOME POINT IN OUR LIVES, MOST OF US HAVE experienced being depressed. Even great men and women of faith in the Bible have experienced depression. For example, Moses went through a period of depression when he became overwhelmed by the responsibility of leading the children of Israel. Elijah became so depressed that he asked God to take his life away. Jeremiah also went through a state of depression because he felt that his preaching was in vain. Martin Luther, the founder of the Protestant Reformation, and other great men of God, have experienced periods of depression. Winston Churchill experienced a depression so deep that he compared it to a black dog that followed him everywhere he went. Abraham Lincoln, one of the greatest presidents in American history, suffered tremendously with depression. All of these individuals were great, but their greatness did not exempt them from depression.

Depression is defined as "to feel sad, dejected, despondent, and melancholy." When people are depressed, everything about them is down, especially their spirits. Depression is another tactic the devil uses to steal Christians' joy and cripple their spirits; he does not want Christians to display the joy of their salvation and shine the light of Christ in this dark world. Satan knows that the world will never be drawn to a depressed witnessed; instead, they'll be repelled by them. He wants us to feel pressed down and be mentally and spiritually bound.

CAUSES OF DEPRESSION

1. Disappointment

One of the causes of depression is disappointment. People become disappointed with other people and situations. Some people are disappointed with their spouses after believing they'd turn out one way, but they later turned out to be different. Some people are disappointed with their

Chapter 5: How To Cope With Depression

children who didn't turn out the way they'd hoped. People also become disappointed when they do not receive promotions on their jobs, when they do not have all of the things they desire, and when the outcomes of situations are not consistent with their expectations. Often times, the devil encourages us to raise the wrong expectations just so that we will be disappointed when things don't happen the way we expect them to. We'll talk more about disappointment in the following chapter.

2. Comparing oneself to others
Another cause of depression is self-comparisons. People often compare themselves to others looking at their possessions and comparing them to that of others, and if they have less than those they are comparing themselves with, they may become depressed. Some people even compare their physical appearances to others: when they notice certain physical features in others which they desire and focus on the fact that they lack those features themselves, they are likely to experience depression.

3. Feeling trapped
Feeling trapped also triggers depression. When people find themselves in situations they cannot get out of, they have a tendency of becoming depressed. This often happens when people are diagnosed with terminally ill diseases or when they find themselves physically limited. People who have lost their hearing or sight, control of their bodies or actual body limbs, they often go through a period of depression even while learning to adjust to their situations.

The feeling of being trapped also occurs in relationships. People are sometimes involved in relationships that they do not feel they can dissolve. Abused women usually find themselves in this situation. They realize that the abuse is not healthy for them, but they are afraid of what their abusers may do if they leave. Abusers often threaten the lives of their victims. Ultimately, many of the victims would prefer to simply live with the abuse rather than die at the hands of their abusers. Many husbands get depressed when in relationships where they feel that their needs are not being met or they are being maliciously attacked and belittled by their wives. Sadly, there are many Christians today who are depressed due to their relationships, believing that they must simply live with abuse of all kinds because someone made them to believe this is a form of "bearing their cross"…which isn't necessarily the case. When people are in relationships that they desire to end but do not feel capable of ending them, they become depressed.

4. Feeling as if one lacks control over a situation
Another trigger for depression is the feeling of losing total control over a situation or situations. Our desire to always be in control is, in essence, due to pride and selfishness. We want what we want when we want it, and if we cannot get what we want, we feel as if the entire world is against us. That is selfishness at its core ("Selfishness" is defined as "concerned excessively or exclusively with oneself: seeking or concentrating on one's own advantage, pleasure, or well-being without regard for others"). Sometimes, God

Chapter 5: How To Cope With Depression

does not give us what we want because our motives are not pure (James 4:3). Instead of desiring to please God, our desire is often to impress man or exalt our own egos. If the glory will not go to God, then the blessing will not come from God. There is no need to be depressed about it! The answer lies in searching the heart and making the intentions pure.

THE DANGERS OF DEPRESSION

1. Damaging healthy relationships

Depressed people do not like to have contact with others. They do not want to go to work, talk with friends, or take care of their responsibilities. Depressed people will watch their phones ring and not even answer the calls that they receive. Being alone is not good for anyone, especially a person who is depressed. Why? Because the devil wants us to be alone so that he can torment our minds and discourage us. When we're around other people who have a positive and godly perspective, they tend to lift us up out of our lowly states and challenge our negative thoughts. Depression breeds isolation, and isolations breeds more depression. It's a vicious cycle of defeat.

2. Suicide

Depression will take away people's desire to live. Many depressed people have considered suicide at some point. It has not occurred to many people that it is in times of disappointment that God is revealing to us what's inside of our hearts, letting us know if we really trust Him as much as we say we do. If God wanted us dead, we would not be here to even consider suicide. God uses disappointments to develop us, not destroy us. Sometimes, God allows situations to occur just to see how we are going to react to them. If we consider suicide, we are saying to God that we do not trust Him and that our situations are too much for Him to handle. Often times, the people in life who accomplish the most are those who have fallen the hardest. Pain and disappointment are teachers, and there's no better way to learn how to be great, do great things, and be strong than to experience low points where you feel like giving up but you persevere anyway (James 1:1-2).

Suicide becomes an escape for those who feel that they can no longer handle life's challenges. Remember, you can take anything as long as God is on your side. There is nothing worth taking you life over. Nothing! You may lose everyone and everything around you, but if you have breath in your body, God knows what you can take. The Bible tells us in 1 Corinthians 10:13 that "there hath no temptation taken you but such as is common to man: but God is faithful." Therefore, we can rest assured that He will "also make a way to escape, that ye may be able to bear it." Thus, it is not necessary for man to seek to escape the things that depress him; it is God who makes that way, and His way is not suicide! The Bible also reminds us in Romans 8:28, "And we know that God causes everything to work together for the good of those who love God and are called according to his purpose for them" (NLT). So, if you continue to trust God in your weakness and heartache and don't give-up on tomorrow, you will end up seeing a better and brighter day.

Chapter 5: How To Cope With Depression

Good things come to those who wait, and brighter days always come to those who trust God, knowing that "weeping may endure for a night, but joy cometh in the morning" (Psalm 30:5).

HOW TO HANDLE DEPRESSION
1. Take control of your emotions/feelings

To handle depression, we must exercise authority over our thoughts and place them under the authority of the Spirit of God as the Bible says in 2 Corinthians 10:5. We cannot let our thoughts have total reign over our lives. When we take control of our thoughts (which we do by speaking God's Word over our lives despite how our situations may look at the moment), we will begin to seize control over our emotions/feelings. What will happen when we do not feel like feeling? We cannot afford to find out the answer to that question. There are some things we have to do whether we *feel* like it or not: one of those things is praise God. We have to give God praise at all times, when things are good and when they are bad, when we are happy and when we are sad. We should praise like David who blessed the Lord at all times, and His praises were continually in his mouth. And the interesting thing about praising God is this: When we praise God, we find our moods changing and lifting. This is because God's presence brings joy and deliverance.

The devil tries to manipulate our feelings and keep us from walking in the will of God. Jesus did not feel like dying. As a matter of fact, Jesus stood in the Garden of Gethsemane and prayed, "Father, if thou be willing, remove this cup from me: nevertheless not my will, but thine be done" (Like 22:24). Jesus knew the devil's tactics. The devil will try and make us focus more on the suffering than the glory that follows the period of suffering. The Word of God tells us "that the sufferings of this present time are not worthy to be compared with the glory which shall be revealed in us" (Romans 8:18).

It is important that we learn to walk in obedience to God and remain faithful to Him regardless of how we feel; after all, God is faithful to us...and He has feelings too. Don't you know God feels sadness, heartache and pain when we disobey Him? The Bible tells us in Ephesians chapter four not to "grieve" the Holy Spirit, which means to bring pain to His heart by engaging in deliberate sin and disobedience. And yet, despite all that we do to God, He gives us life, health and strength every day, He keeps on meeting our needs, and He always makes Himself available to us through prayer.

Here's an example of doing right by God despite how we feel: I was at the doctor's office once and I asked the doctor if he tithed. He told me that he gives according to how he feels. If he feels like giving a hundred dollars, he gives. If he feels like giving twenty dollars, then he gives that. At the end of my visit, I asked him the amount of my bill. He told me that the total was one hundred and fifty dollars. I told him that I only felt like paying twenty-five dollars. Immediately, he said, "I have bills to pay here." I smiled and responded, "I have bills to pay at the church, and I cannot pay those bills based on people giving according to how they feel, just as you cannot pay yours based on

Chapter 5: How To Cope With Depression

how much I feel like paying." He understood my point. None of us can survive by paying according to our feelings. If we did not feel like paying any of our bills one month, we would be out on the street the next. We cannot let feelings control our obeying God. We must obey God out of a pure heart, which means to give when we don't feel like doing so, love when we don't feel like doing so, forgive when we don't feel like doing so, praying, praising and reading His Word when we don't feel like doing so, etc. We don't want God to deal with us based on His feelings, so let's not deal with Him based on ours.

2. Don't focus on the problem, focus on God
When the devil cannot depress us by manipulating our feelings, he attempts to manipulate our minds. He wants us to try and figure out why the things that depress us have taken place in our lives. A lady came to me once to talk about all of the negative occurrences taking place in her life. She said that her parents were dead, her husband had left, and her family was against her. Then she began to question me as to why these things had taken place. I began to minister to her. I told her that she should stop focusing on why things happened and begin to trust God. He is able to bring us out, and He will allow us to get into situations where we have no choice but to trust in Him.

When we trust God, we overcome depression. We may not have all of the answers to our questions, but we have the liberty to praise God and expect our troubles to work together for our good in the end. When I am depressed, I find strength through praising God. As I praise and worship God, I can feel the spirit of depression lifting from me. Never give depression a chance to overtake you. Attack it immediately when you recognize its symptoms. God will bless us when we choose to praise Him in spite of our circumstances. We can look to Job again as an example: Job praised God throughout his trials, and afterwards, "The Lord gave Job twice as much as he had before" (Job 42:10).

The Bible tells us God desires to give His people "beauty for ashes, the oil of joy for mourning, and the garment of praise for the spirit of heaviness..." (Isaiah 61:3). God informed us that praise is a weapon we use to defeat depression. When we praise our way out of depression, we should not look back. Do not wish for what you lost. That only triggers the depression again. Do not wonder about what might have been; consider what shall be. Don't continue to grieve constantly for lost friends and loved ones; focus on those who are with you now and love on them. The past is behind you. Look forward because there are greater things ahead of you!

CHAPTER 6: HOW TO COPE WITH DISAPPOINTMENT

"And the Lord spoke unto Moses that selfsame day, saying, Get thee up into this mountain, Abarim, unto Mount Nebo, which is the land of Moab, that is opposite Jericho; and behold the land of Canaan, which I give unto the children of Israel for a possession." (Deuteronomy 32:48-49).

"And David said to Solomon, My son, as for me, it was in my mind to build A house unto the name of the Lord my God: But the word of the Lord came to me saying, Thou hast shed blood abundantly, and hast made great wars: thou shalt not build a house unto my name, because thou hast shed much blood upon the earth in my sight." (I Chronicles 22:7-8).

Everybody gets disappointed. God gets disappointed. At one point in time, God repented that He made man because...He was disappointed with man. He was disappointed in man's behavior (Genesis 6:6). He had to decide how to handle sin: whether to kill man or to save him. Praise God, He decided to save us.

God saved us from sin, but He didn't save us from disappointment. Disappointments range from the simplest to the most complicated situations. When you plan an outdoor event and it begins to rain, you get disappointed. When an item you have been saving up to purchase goes on sale but ends up getting sold as you approach the counter, you get disappointed. If we fall in love with our dream mate but he or she becomes a living nightmare instead, we get disappointed. If we spend all of our lives loving our children but then they grow up and disown us, we get disappointed. After we give ourselves to the Lord but still wrestle with worldly desires, we tend to get disappointed with ourselves for not being "above temptation". When God heals others but does not heal us, we get disappointed. When God delivers others from smoking, drinking, and other addictions but does not deliver us instantly, we get disappointed.

Not only do we tend to become disappointed with ourselves, but we become disappointed with others as well. Children get disappointed with parents, just as parents get disappointed with their children. When children see parents doing things that they have been taught not to do, they get disappointed. It is not always good to strive to follow in our parents' footsteps, especially when we do not

Chapter 6: How To Cope With Disappointment

know all of the places our parents have been. It is better for us to make our own decisions based off of the Word of God and through prayer when determining the roads we need to take in life. The better roads are usually those less traveled.

DISAPPOINTMENT TEACHES US...

1. How to move on

Often times, God allows disappointments so that He can move us to a new place. Let us use Elijah as an example: Elijah went to Ahab and told him that God was going to stop the rain. After he delivered the message, God sent him to the brook; at the brook, his thirst was quenched until the brook dried up. (I Kings 17:1-7). Elijah's experience shows us that the brook may dry up, even when we are doing the will of God. God allowed Elijah's brook to dry up so that Elijah would be forced to leave and go to another place.

God does not want us to be dependent on just one brook. Occasionally, we become so accustomed to having certain people around us that we cannot function in their absence. We feel that we cannot make it without them in our lives. We rarely consider the possibility that these may be people who were only intended to be in our lives for a reason or a season, not a lifetime. There are storms that come into our lives and God has specific people to help us during those times. He has a group of people to help us during tornado season and another group to help us during hurricane season. Sometimes these people have to be removed from our lives in order for new people to enter in. If we do not let the tornado group go when their season is up, there will be no one to help us through our hurricanes.

2. How not to worship people
Another cause of disappointment in all types of relationships is that we often put people on pedestals. When we place people on pedestals, we create distance between them and ourselves. We should not expect any more of others than we can expect of ourselves. When we do this, we are easily disappointed by their actions. We must remember that no man is above sin, not even those who are being used by God. The men whom God used the most fell in some way. Abraham lied (Genesis 12:13); Lot slept with his daughter; Noah got drunk (Genesis 9:21); David committed adultery and murder (11 Samuel 11). We have to understand that EVERY person is capable of falling! Just as importantly, we must remember that a person who falls is still a child of God and that the gifts and calling of God are without repentance (Romans 11:29).

3. How to trust God
The brooks in our lives are not always people. They may be finances, jobs, education, or any type of situation. Whatever the brook is, God will allow it to dry up, especially if we become more dependent on it than we are on Him. He will allow it to dry up in order to deliver us. It is a blessing, though, that even when one brook dries up, God has another.

Remember the story we discussed in Chapter 4

Chapter 6: How To Cope With Disappointment

about Jesus raising Lazarus from the dead. (John 11). Well, when Mary and Martha first sent for Jesus, Lazarus was just sick. Jesus did not arrive there until four days later. By that time, Lazarus was dead. Mary and Martha were upset with Jesus. When He finally arrived, Martha said to Him, "Lord, if thou hadst been here, my brother had not died" (John 11:21). Why do you think Jesus did not come when Lazarus was sick, but waited until he died? The reason Jesus waited was because He was the only person that could raise Lazarus from the dead.

God will allow the situations you are in to die so that when He raises you up, everybody, including you, will know that He is the only one that could have performed such a miracle. Objects that are dead have a horrible odor to them, which is why no one wants to be around them. Jesus, however, is not afraid of the dead, nor the odor that dead objects exude. He will call you out from that dead situation, whereas, others will only take a whiff of you and then pass you by. After Jesus calls you out and you are washed with the Spirit, those who turned their noses away from you will suddenly wonder how the odor of death became the perfume of life. You will be able to testify that Jesus raised you from your dead situation. Nothing and no one will be able to receive credit for what He has done! It will not be because of looks, or education, or finances, or intellect, or family, or friends; it will be because of the power of the Lord God Almighty that you made it! Even if God does not show up when you want Him to show up, He will be there on time.

A lot of times we get disappointed with God's timing. We don't like the amount of time that it takes for God to make us who He wants us to be. All of Moses' life he had difficulty. God took eight years to make Moses into the man He needed him to be to lead the children of Israel (Exodus 2, 3). God spent more time making Moses than He did using him—Moses only led the Israelites for forty years. We don't always understand God takes so long to do certain things in our lives, but God has a purpose for doing things the way that He does.

It may take God years to prepare you to complete one assignment He has for you. Let us consider the making of a good husband and a good father: The time that a man spends hungry and with little finances teaches him how to live without and survive on little so that when he gets married and becomes responsible for his wife and children he will know how to withstand difficult times without giving up and also prioritize concerning the family finances.

When God allows people to be single for a lengthy period of time, He is preparing them for marriage so that their marriages will last. When people have been single for a long time, they will not allow the devil to just step I and destroy their relationships with the mates God has given them. They will stand by their mates, encouraging them and supporting them in every situation. They will not compare their mates to others because they realize that God gives His children exactly what we need. God knows the kind of person that you need in your life; and if you wait on Him, He will give you that person. There will be no need for you to go out of your normal character to impress your chosen mate. He or she will be impressed with

Chapter 6: How To Cope With Disappointment

you just the way you are because God has already prepared them to receive the REAL you.

HOW TO HANDLE DISAPPOINTMENT

The way we deal with disappointment is important to God. Throughout the forty years that Moses led the children of Israel, there were many times that he was disappointed with their actions. For instance, when Moses came down from the mountain after receiving the Ten Commandments from God, he found the people worshipping a golden calf. He became so angry that he threw the tablets down and broke them (Exodus 32:19). Even though Moses had led the children of Israel as God had instructed, God told Moses "Because ye trespassed against me…and ye sanctified me not…Yet thou shalt see the land before thee; but thou shalt not go thither unto the land which I give the children of Israel" (Deuteronomy 32:51-52).

In 1 Chronicles 22, we find that David, a man after God's own heart, was not able to build the Lord a temple because he had "shed blood abundantly." David was disappointed that he could not fulfill his dream of building a house for God. Sometimes God allows us to be disappointed so that He can give others a chance. Young people will never be able to do anything for God if older people try to do everything and never give them a chance. God wants everyone to take part in building His temple. The idea of the temple was David's, but it was his son, Solomon, who God allowed to build it. We have to be willing to give others a chance. Do not disappoint someone else because you have been disappointed.

Coping with the Uncopable

When we are disappointed, we should not stop moving forward. If one thing does not work out in our favor, we must move on to something new. We should go to God and ask Him to show us the lesson that we are to learn from our disappointment. We cannot focus on the disappointment—it is over! All we can do is simply learn the lesson so we won't repeat it. If we do not bury the past, it will bury us. We have to focus on our present situations and ask God which direction to go. When we leave our disappointments from the past in the past, we make ourselves available for God to lead us into our futures!

CHAPTER 7: HOW TO COPE WITH FEAR

*"For God hath not given us the spirit of fear;
but of power, and of love, and of a sound mind."*
(11 Timothy 1:7)

No person is exempt from fear. Everybody is afraid of something. People do not always admit their fears, but they have them. Julius Caesar was a great emperor, but he was afraid of lightning. Whenever storms came, he would hide under his bed. The source of fear differs from person to person.

Some people are afraid of losing their friends, families, and material possessions—they do not want to be alone. Some people are afraid of criticism—they do not want people to say anything about them. Some are afraid of aging—they do not want to be unable to care for themselves. Some people are afraid of taking risks—they do not want to lose what they already have. Though the types of fear are different, they share common causes.

CAUSES OF FEAR

1. A Controlling Spirit

One cause of fear is the desire to be in control of everything. Elijah was a mighty man of God, but he was afraid of Jezebel because he could not control her. He was able to call fire down from heaven, but he was not able to keep her from his trail. He was so afraid of Jezebel that he asked God to take his life. (1 Kings 19,20).

2. Guilt

Guilt is another cause of fear. When a person is guilty, his or her conscience bothers them. The first time fear appears in the Bible is when Adam was hiding from God because he had sinned. It is ironic that Adam attempted to hide himself behind a tree, since a tree played a major part in his downfall. When God came looking for Adam, Adam was afraid because he was guilty.

3. Ignorance

When people are ignorant about something, they tend to be fearful of it. This contributes to the prevalence of racism in this country. People are afraid of ethnicities other than their own because they have been told something negative about that group. If the groups actually took the time to learn about each other, they would find that they have no reason to be afraid. People are just people.

Chapter 7: How To Cope With Fear

4. Worrying about others' opinions
Believing what people say about you can cause you to become afraid. If you were walking down the street and someone told you that you did not look well, you would be afraid that something might be wrong with you. If you met another person who mentioned your appearance as well, you would be afraid that something is wrong with you. As a result, you'd probably go home, get in the bed, and begin taking medicine, not because you feel sick, but because somebody else said you looked sick.

Sometimes, people tell you negative things about yourself because they feel threatened by you. Just because a person says something negative (or positive) about you does not mean that it is true. You know yourself better than anybody . . . except God. Don't believe everything that others say. Believe what you know and what God has told you.

Fear will cause you to forget who you are and what you know to be true. Once, a lady began to run through the streets of a city, exclaiming, "The dam is broken!" People began to run out of their homes and join her, chanting to all those they passed, "The dam is broken!" They passed by the house of an old man and he joined them as well. After they had gone about ten miles, the old man yelled for everyone to stop. He said, "Wait! I have been living here for sixty-five years, there is no dam in this city!!" He and the others had been so caught up in the excitement of the moment that they did not realize the absurdity of it.

4. Worry

Worry is another cause of fear. Some people love to worry; they are filled with paranoia, forgetting or not realizing that most of things that we worry about never take place. Some men who worry about where their wives are when they are not at home, and they allow the enemy to begin to put the thought in their heads that their wives are with someone else. Some women worry that every time their husbands leave the house they are going to leave them—when all they're going to is the grocery store. When people worry about things that have not taken place, they become afraid of the things they have imagined, things which are far from reality.

Once, there was a man who stopped to give an old lady a ride. He asked the lady her name, and she told him her name was Disease. Immediately, he told her she would have to get out. She promised him that if he would let her ride, she would only kill ten people in his town. He agreed. The next day, the local paper printed that one hundred people had died from Disease. The man went to the woman to confront her. She listened and then responded, "I kept my word. I only killed ten people, but when the other ninety heard about me, they were so afraid that they worried themselves to death."

A HEALTHY FEAR TO HAVE

The only fear we should have is the fear of the Lord, because the fear of "the Lord is the beginning of wisdom" (Psalm 111:10). This does not mean that we should look upon the Lord as an unapproachable entity, but it does

Chapter 7: How To Cope With Fear

mean that we should reverence and respect Him. Any form of fear we experience other than the fear of the Lord is not of God, but of the devil. We know this because the Bible says, "God has not given us the spirit of fear" (11 Timothy 1:7). The devil uses fear to control our actions. Most people who do not give and support ministries are afraid that they cannot afford to do so. They are afraid that if they tithe and plant seed offerings, they will not be able to pay all of their bills. They are afraid to trust God who has already promised that if you bring the tithes into His storehouse, He will "open you the windows of heaven, and pour you out a blessing, that there shall not be room enough to receive it" (Malachi 3:10). If God has given us His word, there is no need to fear.

When Jesus began to walk toward the disciples on the Sea of Galilee, "they were troubled, saying, it is a spirit; and they cried out in fear" (Matthew 14:26). Jesus spoke to them and said, "Be not afraid" (Matthew 14:28). Peter began walking on the water. But as he drew near to Jesus, he suddenly began to sink. What happened to cause him to begin to sink being so close to Jesus? He began to sink because he took his eyes off of Jesus and focus on the winds and waves of the sea all around him. The Bible says, "...when he saw the wind boisterous, he as afraid" (Matthew 14:30).

We should never take our eyes off of Jesus because He walks on the things that drown us, and if we trust Him and continue to focus on Him, He'll empower us to walk on those things, too. What keeps us from walking on our situations is the fact that we keep losing focus on God and instead, we began to focus more on our health, our finances, and the people around us. We tend to forget that God can handle every situation. There is no need for us to lose sleep due to fear. The God we serve "shall never slumber nor sleep" (Psalms 121:4). Why should we stay awake all night worrying when God is already awake and watching over us? If we ever decide within ourselves to place our eyes on Him despite the things that are happening around us, we will be able to walk on our situations without sinking in them—then, and then only, will we find rest.

HOW TO HANDLE FEAR

First, in order to handle fear, we must accept reality. By this, I mean we must accept the reality that we are not in control of everything and only God is truly in control of everything. When we learn to relinquish control of every situation to God, we will become less paranoid and fearful of the outcome, knowing that with God all things are working together for our good and for His glory. The more you try to control people and circumstances, the more you fall under the power of fear. We defeat fear by trusting God with our lives, our families, our finances, etc. Now, I'm not saying we abandon wisdom and commonsense. Sure, we learn to budget, eat right, take safety measures to protect ourselves and our families, but we also accept that fact that beyond that which we are capable of, we can only trust God to take care of the rest. Relax. God is in control.

Another thing we must do in order to defeat fear is to turn to God's Word for comfort. If you find yourself in situations that are causing you to have fear, go to your

Chapter 7: How To Cope With Fear

favorite Bible passages and begin reading them. My favorite passage is in Psalms 27. The Lord is my light and my salvation; whom shall I fear? The Lord is the strength of my life; of whom shall I be afraid? When the wicked, even mine enemies and my foes, come upon me to eat up my flesh, they stumbled and fell. Though a host should encamp against me, my heart shall not fear: Thou war should rise up against me, in this will I be confident (Palm 27: 1-3). Whenever I am facing difficult situations, I begin reading this passage. When the enemy sends rear my way, I can overcome it because I have the Word to stand on. The word is my reminder that I have no need to fear!

Coping with the Uncopable

CHAPTER 8: HOW TO COPE WITH HURT

*"Lord, who shall abide in thy tabernacle?
Who shall dwell in thy holy hill?" (Psalms 15:1).*

*"In whose eyes a vile person is contemned;
But honoreth them that fear the Lord.
He that sweareth to his own hurt and changeth
not." (Psalms 15:4)*

WE LIVE IN A WORLD FILLED WITH HURTING people and many of those people are in the church. There are a variety of reasons why people feel pain—broken relationships, unfulfilled promises, and unexpected disappointments are only a few of the things that hurt people. Pain is a universal emotion, but its causes are individual. What may cause one person pain might not necessarily cause another person pain; therefore, we will not concentrate on the specifics of what causes people pain, but we will deal with why God allows us to be hurt and how we should handle the pain of being hurt.

GOD ALLOWS US TO EXPERIENCE PAIN TO...
1. Protect us

People often wonder why a living God would allow people to experience pain. Well, there are several reasons He allows it, and they are all beneficial to His people. People may find this difficult to accept, but sometimes God allows us to get hurt as a way of protecting us. By allowing us to feel one type of pain, He may be protecting us from a deeper pain. Sometimes, God allows us to get hurt by people early in certain relationships to protect us from a greater hurt that would have occurred had the relationship lasted longer. Your engagement to a particular person may have been broken off simply because that was not the person God intended for you to marry. You may have thought they were the right person, but God knows better than you who the right person really is; therefore, He allowed the person you chose to hurt you so that He could present you with the person He chose. It was His way of protecting you from a bigger hurt up the road.

2. Move us

God also allows us to get hurt because He wants to do something new in our lives, and, in order to do this, He has to get us out of our nests, which are our comfort zones. The only way He can get us out is to tear up the nests that

Chapter 8: How To Cope With Hurt

we have built. We like to stay in the nests because we do not have to do anything new, different, or challenging when we are in our nests; we don't have to push ourselves to higher heights and step out on faith. The mother eagle will go out and get everything the eaglets need, and then bring it back to the nest. Eventually, though, the mother eagle will stir the nest so that the eaglets will become uncomfortable within the nest; she does this so that her eaglets will stop depending on her, learn to spread their own wings, and fly; she does this because she knows that storms will come, and that if everyone doesn't learn to be responsible for themselves they will all perish in the storms.

God stirs our nests with pain when He is ready for us to branch out into something new and also mature. He does not want us to depend on people, but He wants us to depend on Him. When people begin to hurt us, we realize that God is the only one we can depend on totally to supply all of our needs. God wants us to know that we truly can make it without some people. We will not know this until the people are gone from our lives.

I depended a lot on my son, Aric, who was killed in a car accident. He was my best friend. We laughed, talked, and shared things with each other that we had not shared with any other person. He was my first-born son, the child of my youth. We had a special bond because we grew up together—my wife and I married and conceived him while still very young. My son died while in the prime of his ministry, and I was crushed by his sudden death.

God revealed to me that my son had actually become my prop, and when God allowed him to be taken from me, I felt a hurt that I had never felt before; but God was there to comfort me, and I learned to lean on Him again. There are people in our lives that we feel we cannot live without, but when they die, we then discover that we can live without them.

3. Mature us

God allows us to get hurt because pain, as a teacher, matures us. When we look back over our educational careers, we usually remember the lessons we learned from the teachers who were the hardest on us and caused us the most stress. When we attempt to teach children certain lessons, we teach them by using pain. For example, you may tell a child several times not to touch the stove because it is hot; and yet, it is not until they touch it and feel the pain that they learn the lesson.

Paul prayed to God for power, and God gave him a thorn in his flesh (1 Corinthians 12:7). Many times we ask for pleasant things, but God gives us painful things instead. Why is this? It is because God knows what we need, and He knows that pain is one of the things we need: pain usually drives us to God and into our destinies. When we are hurting, we spend more time with God. We pray more earnest prayers and study God's Word more diligently when we are seeking relief. If that hurt was not in your life, you would probably ignore God.

4. Teach us compassion

People who are experiencing great pain sometimes set out to hurt others. They do this because they want people to

Chapter 8: How To Cope With Hurt

feel what they are feeling. If you do not respond to their pain when they express it to you, they'll then try to inflict in on you, thinking that you will understand them better. People do not like it when the things that cause them hurt do not cause others to hurt, and as a result, people will search to discover the things that will hurt you; they want to break you because they fell broken; they are angered by your strength, because it magnifies what they feel is their weakness. I know this sounds strange, but it is normal to feel this way. We were created by God to socialize and connect on an emotional level. We were created to empathize and sympathize with one another. Pain helps us to establish this type of human connection and bonding. When a person is hurt, identifying with their hurt and showing compassion towards them will cause them to further connect with you, and in some cases, this may mean the difference between life and death: it may prevent a person from taking their own life and/or the life of another person.

HOW TO HANDLE HURT

Most husbands who are abusive to their wives are suffering from personal hurt and pain. Unfortunately, they have not been taught proper coping methods. The only reason they strike out at their wives is that they want them to feel pain because they feel it. When spouses turn away from each other and ignore and neglect each other, they do so because they know that it will hurt each other; they do this because they are hurting, and they want their spouse to hurt as well. Instead of perpetuating a cycle of pain, we need to reach out and comfort one another so that healing can take place. Divorces are caused as a result of two people neglecting each other to the point that they no longer communicate; they develop a pattern of neglect and abuse that becomes more difficult to break because they allowed it to continue to so long. Break the cycle of neglect and abuse early.

We must learn how to deal with the pain that others inflict on us by seeking to understand the one inflicting it. When Jesus was hanging on the cross, He said, "Father forgive them for they know not what they do." Jesus was expressing the reason for the pain His persecutors was inflicting on Him: they were ignorant. Know why people do what they do helps us to handle the pain caused by their actions a lot more. When I first began preaching (at the age of 11), my dad would never come out to hear me preach. He hated church. I felt saddened by this. But, later on in life, when I went back to my dad's hometown and discovered why he hated church so much—it was due to his mother's funeral not being allowed in her home church because she hadn't paid her dues—I began to understand him and feel less hurt by his actions. My hurt then turned into sympathy and compassion.

Another thing we should keep in mind is the fact that not only have others hurt us, but we have also hurt others. Sometimes, we focus so much on what others have done to us that we forget what we have done to others. So someone broke your heart. Have you forgotten about the person's heart you broke? So someone lied on you. Have you forgotten about the lies you told on others? Remember what God forgave you of and it will be easy for you to

Chapter 8: How To Cope With Hurt

overcome the hurt someone else caused you.

Lastly, when we are trying to handle the pain that others have caused us we should consider Proverbs 24:17-18, which tells us to "rejoice not when thine enemy falleth, and let not thine heart be glad when he stumbleth: Lest the Lord see it, and it displease him, and he turn away his wrath from him." When we rejoice at the pain and suffering of those who have caused us pain, God becomes angry with us. Instead of rejoicing, we should pray for their deliverance. Why? Because, rather than give us our just due, God granted us mercy. What if God gave us what we truly deserve?

The best way to deal with the pain people have caused is to choose to "love your enemies" (Luke 6:27). When you love others in spite of what they have done to you, you teach them what it means to be a Christian, and you also overcome evil. Your love for them will point them in the direction of Christ because they will recognize that there has to be a greater power that gives you the strength to love them even though they have caused you so much pain. It is not you that gives you the strength to love them, but the power within you that controls you. When you allow God to empower you love those who hurt you, that same power will heal the pain that they caused you. Ultimately, the hurtful experience has given God glory!

Coping with the Uncopable

CHAPTER 9: HOW TO COPE WITH INSECURITY

"And Moses said unto God, Who am I, that I should go unto Pharaoh?" (Exodus 3:11)

WHEN GOD CAME TO MOSES AND INFORMED him that He wanted him to go before Pharaoh and deliver the children of Israel out of Egypt, Moses asked God, "Who am I, that I should go unto Pharaoh, and that I should bring forth the children of Israel out of Egypt?" (Exodus 3:11). Moses asked this because he was insecure. He did not feel worthy of completing the task that God was assigning to him. He began to explain to God that he had a speech problem. There was no need for him to tell God this because God already knew it—God knew it before Moses ever spoke his first word. God assured Moses that his speech impediment would not interfere with what He was telling him to do. God already made sure that Moses had what he needed to complete the assignment. Moses still was unsure of this calling, so God told Moses to cast down his rod. When the rod hit the ground it turned into a serpent (Exodus 4:3). God then instructed Moses to pick the snake up by the tail, and once he did so, the snake turned back into a rod. God wanted Moses to know that He was in control and that He was able to work through him if he would simply yield to Him and obey. This is the same challenge we often face in life. We must, likewise, learn how to overcome our personal insecurities and step out on faith and in obedience to God's instructions. Here are the signs of insecurity which we must face and overcome:

SIGNS OF INSECURITY

1. Always needing other people around

One sign of insecurity is that a person only feels secure when around other people. Gang members are a prime example of this. As long as they are around their fellow gang members, they will confidently steal, kill, and destroy, but when you find them alone, they have very little to say and even less to do. This is because they do not have the protection of the other gang members. They are secure around others, but they are not secure within themselves.

2. Jealousy

Jealousy is another sign of insecurity. A jealous spouse always want to know where the other is and what he or she is doing at all times. This would be fine if they wanted to

Chapter 9: How To Cope With Insecurity

know out of genuine concern, but it becomes a problem when they are concerned about their partner's whereabouts for the purpose of controlling them. An insecure man does not want his wife to talk to any other man because he is afraid that the other person may be interested in her. As a matter of fact, he does not want her to do anything or leaving his sight at all out of fear of losing her to another man. If he could go to work with her, he would. The same is to be said about an insecure wife...or an insecure person in general. A person who is secure, however, does not worry about who their spouse talks to or where they go because they are confident that their spouse loves them and that no one can take what they have.

3. Competition

Insecure people are often competitive. They work hard to keep up with what other people are doing. They are never satisfied with what they have and are always comparing themselves to others. At work, they compete with their colleagues, and at home, they compete with their family members and friends. Many strive to be perfectionists because they do not want people to have any negative opinions about them. They are usually in and out of relationships because they are not comfortable with themselves, and they are trying to be who they think the other person wants them to be and not who they really are. In the process of developing their personality, they compete with the personalities of those they are involved with. They only feel a sense of worth when sizing themselves up next to other people.

4. Antisocial

Many insecure people do not feel comfortable around other people. The woman Jesus met at the well in John chapter 4 was an insecure woman—I know this because of the time that she went to the well to draw water: she went at noon; but in those days, women went to the well early in the morning or late in the evening. This woman was also alone although it was customary for women to go to the wells in groups. This woman's insecurities were a result of the lifestyle that she lived. She knew that people discussed the fact that she had five husbands and was currently with a man who was not her husband. She knew she was the talk of the town, the subject of much gossip. To keep from dealing with people, she would visit the well at the hottest time of the day. This shows just how determined she was to avoid being around others, and this also reveals just how much she was controlled by her insecurities. After she met Jesus, her insecurities gave way to boldness, and she went about facing the very people she tried to avoid and telling them about *the man* that she had met—the man who revealed the issues of her heart and changed her life during a single conversation: Jesus.

5. Low self-esteem

Insecure people are easily intimidated by others due to their negative perception of themselves. People who are insecure about their bodies allow their bodies to determine not only what they wear, but how they carry themselves as well. Overweight people who are insecure tend

Chapter 9: How To Cope With Insecurity

to wear their clothes larger than necessary in an effort to camouflage their actual size. They do not wear anything or do anything that draws attention to them because they assume that the attention will be negative. They find it difficult to believe that someone will be interested in them romantically because they've been conditioned to believe that thin is in and stout is out; and as a result of this, they look unapproachable not because they are not willing to be approached, but because they do not believe that they will be approached. They are being controlled by their negative perceptions of themselves and are projecting their own thoughts on to others when in reality what they are thinking may not be what others are thinking.

6. A lack of confidence
People who are insecure about themselves often do not make an effort to pursue the things that they desire in life. They believe they are not capable of obtaining them, nor worthy of receiving them. For instance, an insecure man who is interested in a woman may never approach her because he does not think that he will be received by her. He may be insecure over the fact that she is an educated and independent woman who is secure within herself and automatically assumes that such a woman has a host of men interested in her and that she will not respond to him because he does not have all of the same things that she has. He is intimidated by the number of degrees she has, the amount of money she makes, the kind of car she drives, and the house that she lives in. What he doesn't realize is that woman is really lonely and desirous not of a rich man

or a man with a long list of degrees, but of a man who is secure within himself, knows how to respect and treat a lady right, and loves God. He doesn't realize that she actually wants him to show an interest in her. Her concern is not what he has, but what he wants to have. However, the fact that he is insecure in his present state causes him to miss a wonderful opportunity. We must overcome insecurities in order to strive for those things which we desire.

A large number of single people are insecure because they do not have a mate. There is nothing wrong with being single, nor does being single mean that there is something wrong with you. Adam was single before God gave him Eve. As Adam went about doing what God instructed him to do, God saw that Adam was lonely and proceeded to create Eve. If you are a single person, you should not concentrate on the fact that you are alone; instead, you should focus on serving God and improving in the areas of your life that need improving. When you are spending your time working for God, He will acknowledge what you need in life. God already knows what we both want and need in life and will provide these things for us in due season. Do not be insecure because you are single. Be secure in the fact that God has prepared a mate specifically for you.

6. Comparing oneself
People who are insecure in their salvation compare themselves to other Christians. They observe other Christians and constantly wish that they could be like them. They envy those who speak in tongues, appear to live holy, or

Chapter 9: How To Cope With Insecurity

have some extraordinary spiritual gift. They are not aware, however, of all of the difficulty the people they desire to be like are experiencing, and neither do they consider the possibility that their lifestyles may be as holy, if not holier, than those people they are comparing themselves with. They forget that no one is perfect or sinless. Just because God has gifted someone or chose to use them in a particular office doesn't mean that person is any better than anyone else; it just means that person was willing to allow God to use him or her; nonetheless, even those who're used by God experience difficulties in their Christian lives.

Likewise, this is the case in life in general. Many people envy and compare themselves to others who have money, fame, success, etc., but don't count the cost that these people had to pay in order to get what they have. Insecurity blinds us to the reality of struggle: that no good thing in life comes without some type of struggle. The rich have to work hard to get where they are and work even harder to remain there. The successful had to shed blood, sweat, and tears just to get where they are. Many successful people get little rest and work more hours than the average person. For example, a regular employee may work 40 hours a week to get a paycheck, but a medical doctor may work up to 70 hours a week in order to get by, and with that, they may rarely see or spend time with their families, or in some cases, be able to really spend time enjoying the wealth they've obtained. Never compare yourself to another person unless you know the struggle that person has undergone or is undergoing and unless you are willing to make the same sacrifices in life to get to where that person is.

7. Constantly need the praises of other people
Everyone needs affirmation and validation in life, but insecure people constantly need others to affirm them. It seems as if they can never get enough. For example, an insecure wife needs her husband to tell her constantly that he loves her. There is nothing wrong with a man telling his wife that he loves her, but if she needs him to tell her ten times a day, then she is suffering with an insecurity. If she overcomes her insecurity, she will be able to recognize his love for her, even if it goes unsaid. An insecure husband constantly tries to remind and prove to his wife that he is the man of the house. If he were truly the man of the house and confident in that position, he wouldn't have to say that he is the man of the house and throw his ego around even to the point of not including his wife in his decision-making process just to prove that his word is law and he reigns supreme. Everything that he does, including discussing situations with his wife, understanding that he is obligated by God to share with his wife in the decision-making process according to 1 Peter 3:7, would exemplify that he is the man of the house. He won't need to constantly remind her of his position and she will naturally respect him simply because he's doing what he supposed to do because God said to do it rather than doing it because he wants to prove a point to her. She'll know that he'll be responsible whether she supports him or not.

HOW TO HANDLE INSECURITY

Chapter 9: How To Cope With Insecurity

If a person is battling with insecurity, he or she needs to obtain knowledge. The majority of our insecurities are a result of a lack of knowledge. If we do not understand ideas, concepts, situations, people, and especially ourselves, our families, our culture, and our history, we will develop a sense of insecurity. When people do not know who they are, they have difficulty accepting and appreciating who they are and this causes them to be easily intimidated by others. But when people are confidant in who they are, they do not let others intimidate them.

Saul tried to intimidate David when he showed up to kill Goliath. He told David that he was too young and too small to face the massive Goliath. David did not allow this to bother him. He knew that he was capable of killing the giant because he knew that God was with him. God had already proven himself to David by enabling David to kill a bear and a lion (1 Samuel 17). When people remember what God has already done for them, they won't be moved by what people say; instead, they'll be moved by the fact that God is with them. What we know about God from experience supersedes our insecurities and releases an anointing that will equip us to overcome any obstacle.

In order to have the kind of confidence that David had, Christians must realize that, as the body is one but has many members, the same goes for the body of Christ (1 Corinthians 12:12). We should not be jealous and intimidated by each other because God did not design us to do the same thing; He designed us individually and equipped each of us for the battles that we have been chosen to fight. Our focus should be on preparing for our own personal battles and to accomplish God's will for our individual lives; instead, however, we tend to look at the way others prepare and compare our training, gifts, and callings to theirs. We forget that they are training for an entirely different fight. Once everyone focuses on training for their own fight, they will lose sight of the things that make them feel insecure and become secure in knowing that they can win the battles through God's power that they have specifically been called by God to fight; they will know that they have a purpose, an assignment, a reason for living all their own and realize that their significance is in completing their assignment and doing God's will for their own life. When everyone fights his or her assigned battles, the entire body of Christ will win the war!

CHAPTER 10: HOW TO COPE WITH LONELINESS

"Now the Lord of peace himself gives you peace always by all means. The Lord be with you all." (11 Thessalonians 3:16)

Most of us might not consider ourselves to be lonely because we have family and friends around us, but we must consider the fact that we can be lonely in the midst of a crowd. Loneliness is not a physical state of being, but rather, it is a state of mind. It is not determined by your physical location, but your mental situation. There is a difference in aloneness and loneliness. Some people are alone but not lonely, and some are lonely, though not alone.

Just as people in crowds can be lonely, people who are by themselves may not necessarily be lonely: they are simply alone. There is a difference between the two. Everyone needs some time to themselves. Jesus spent much time alone (Luke 9:18, 36). There is nothing wrong with being alone at times; the problem is when we remain isolated and become lonely.

WHAT CAUSES LONELINESS?
1. Focusing on ourselves
There are several things that cause people to feel lonely. Surprising enough, many times, we are the source of our own loneliness. For example, our pride keeps us isolated and feeling lonely. Excessive pride is the reason Satan will forever be isolated from God. He was so proud himself because of the gifts and his beauty which God had given him that he said, "I will ascend into heaven, I will exalt my throne above the stars of God: I will sit also upon the mount of the congregation, in the sides of the north: I will ascend above the heights of the clouds; I will be like the most High" (Isaiah 14:13-15).

People who are excessively proud and arrogant tend to think of themselves as being superior to other people; they do not feel like they need other people, and as a result of this thinking, they drive other people away from them. Eventually, their state of aloneness becomes loneliness, and their isolation causes them to quickly realize that they actually do need other people. Sadly, their pride and arrogance creates a wall that blocks them from connecting and valuing other people based on genuine characteristics so that they can develop healthy relationships, and often times, this wall of pride is due to the way they have been

Chapter 10: How To Cope With Loneliness

treated by other people in the past.

2. Thinking you are always right
Sometimes loneliness comes as a result of us pushing people away due to your thinking you are always right and no one else knows anything. Some parents are lonely because they have pushed their children away, being unwilling to accept the fact that their children are adults and that they can and must make decisions for themselves. These overbearing parents constantly try to tell their grown children how to live their lives and even become offended when their children choose to do things their way. As a result of this, their children do not include them in on their struggles because they do not want to be told what to do. Parents have to understand that they have to let their children live their own lives, and simply love them even when they make mistakes. God will do the rest! Do not be a cause of your own loneliness.

In marriages, when one spouse is constantly treating their partner as if they aren't allowed to have an opinion in the relationship or as if they are inferior, they will end up being lonely in a marriage. When we are overbearing and unwilling to allow our partners to freely speak and express their feelings without being interrupted and cut off then the communication will become strained and eventually dry up and we will find ourselves living in a cold household with a person that has become a perfect stranger. We must realize that we are not always right and that God has placed other people in our lives with the answers and the help that we need—because no one is self-sufficient and can survive entirely on their own in this world.

3. Living to please others

People who try to live up to the expectations of others are often lonely. When people long to be but cannot be who other people want them to be, they'll distance themselves out of frustration. The reason people try to be who others expect them to be is because they are insecure within themselves. Sometimes, the expectations that they are attempting to live up to are not really the expectations of others, but they are expectations that they have created in their own minds but are projecting onto others. In either case, living up to the expectations of others, real or imagined, will always lead to loneliness because we can only be who we truly are. Any attempt to be someone other than ourselves will only be short-lived. This is not to say that we cannot change things about ourselves, but we must understand that we CANNOT change the essence of who we are.

4. Feeling forgotten of unwanted

Loneliness occurs when people feel forgotten and unwanted. Everyone wants to feel loved and needed. Everyone wants to feel appreciated. Children sometimes feel lonely because their parents spend very little time with them. They may have all of the latest in toys, games, and clothes, but "things" cannot replace relationships. When children feel unwanted at home, they look to others, usually their peers, for that attention; the attention they receive from their peers may excite them, but it may not be positive.

Chapter 10: How To Cope With Loneliness

But many children are led astray because they are simply glad to receive attention, any attention, and they will do whatever it takes to keep it, including things they have been taught not to do, things they know are wrong. They do this to avoid being lonely.

5. Losing someone close

The death of a loved one can also cause people to feel lonely. When people have become a part of our lives, it is difficult for us to accept the fact that they are gone forever. We feel lonely without them because they can never be replaced. Even though it is healthy for us to grieve, we should not forever remain in a state of loneliness. We have to think about the people that are still a part of our lives. When a man or woman loses a spouse, it is important that they don't allow loneliness to overwhelm them and cause them to forget about the children who are left and who need their attention. When I lost my son, I had to remember that I still had other sons who needed me and a grandson who also needed a father-figure. I wouldn't have been able to fulfill my duties as a father and grandfather if I didn't get past the loneliness I felt as a result of my son's death. In times of loss, if we remember what we have left, we will not succumb to a state of loneliness.

6. Having a pity-party

Self-pity is another cause of loneliness. Elijah, the prophet, experienced this. When Jezebel threatened him, he ran into the wilderness "and he requested for himself that he might die; and said, it is enough; now, O Lord, take away my life; for I am not better than my fathers" (1 Kings 19:4). Elijah was having a pity party because he thought that he was the only man of God who remained. God had to remind him that there were others who had not bowed down to Baal, and then called him out of the cave he was hiding in and sent him back to work. Get over your pity party because...you still have a job to do.

7. Exalting your personal experiences above other's
Many of us feel lonely because we think that we are the only people who are experiencing problems. We think that we are the only people who are sick, lack money, feel weary, and are struggling mentally and emotionally with something. We are not! Other people experience the same things we do, even if no one wants to admit it. We believe that people will think less of us if they know what we are going through when actually, our testimonies may just help them to make it through their personal trials. We are not alone in our struggles! We all have them. The Bible tells us "there hath no temptation taken you but such as is common to man" (1 Corinthians 10:13). This is confirmation that we are not alone. Our experiences are common to all men; so, don't act like you're the only one going through something or that no one else understands your struggle.

8. Sin
Another cause of loneliness is sin. Why? Because sin separates us from God, and when we are in a state of spiritual separation from God, we feel a sense of shame. After we

Chapter 10: How To Cope With Loneliness

sin, we do not feel worthy to go before God. We are afraid to ask for forgiveness, especially when we have committed a sin that we have already been forgiven for. When we are in this state, we long to come back to God, but our shame keeps us away from Him.

The further we move away from God, the lonelier we become. We are lonely because there is a part of us that automatically desires to be connected with God. God designed us with an automatic void built on the inside of us that makes us long for His presence. But in order for us to be restored and returned unto Him, we must humble ourselves and ask for forgiveness. And no, we are not worthy of God's forgiveness, but that is exactly why He gives us grace. We should not allow sin to trap us in loneliness. God is waiting for us, saying, "I have blotted out, as a thick cloud, thy transgressions, and, as a cloud, they sins: return unto me; for I have redeemed thee" (Isaiah 44:22).

DEALING WITH LONELINESS

Loneliness is a state of mind; therefore, the only way to handle it is by changing the way we think. If we change the way we think, we will automatically change the way we act. If we stop thinking that we are better than other people, they will not steer away from us; they will instead draw nearer to us. If we stop thinking that we must live up to the expectations of others and instead concentrate on meeting God's expectations, we won't feel the need to distance ourselves from people. If we recognize that we are not the only ones who have problems we won't feel that others don't understand us; instead, we will know that we have someone to share our testimonies with. These testimonies will help us defeat the state of loneliness.

More than anything, we must not allow sin to keep us separated from God. Once we ask God to forgive us for our sins, our relationship with Him will automatically be restored. "Therefore if any man be in Christ, he is a new creature: old things are passed away; behold, all things are become new" (11 Corinthians 5:17). Even still, God has never turned His back on us just because we sinned. For, the Bible declares that He is "married to the backslider" (Jeremiah 3:14). That means God is always waiting for us to repent. He doesn't walk away because we fell. When no one else is around, God will be there. We can count on God at all times; and if we are in fellowship with Him, WE ARE NEVER ALONE!

CHAPTER 11: HOW TO COPE WITH OPPOSITION

"And Judah said, the strength of bearers of the burdens is decayed, and there is much rubbish; so that we are not able to build the wall. And our adversaries said, they shall not know, neither see, till we come in the midst among them and slay them, and cause the work of cease. And it came to pass that when the Jews which dwelt by them came, they said unto us ten times, From all places whence ye shall return unto us they will be upon you. Therefore set I in the lower places behind the wall, and on the higher places, I even set the people after their families with their swords, their spears, and their bows. And I looked, and rose up, and said unto the nobles, and to the rulers, and to the rest of the people, Be not ye afraid of them; remember the Lord, which is great and terrible, and fight for your brethren, your sons, and

your daughters, your wives, and your houses. And it came to pass, when our enemies heard that it was known unto us, and God had brought their counsel to naught, that we returned all of us to the wall, every-one unto his work (Nehemiah 4:10-15)

PEOPLE WHO ARE WORKING TOWARDS A particular goal usually have some type of opposition facing them. Whenever a person is attempting to do something that will bring God glory, Satan will attack them using opposition. If there is no opposition in your life, then maybe you are not working on anything significant enough to make the devil mad or concerned. Every Christian should know that they will have opposition in this world. Do not be fooled into thinking that everyone will like you, understand you, and appreciate you. You are going to face opposition!

PREPARING FOR OPPOSITION

Satan opposes Christians because he recognizes the anointing that rests upon their lives. Satan constantly reminds us of our pasts. He wants us to feel guilty about things that we have done, which God has already forgiven us of. Satan also opposes us by reminding us of our imperfections—he hopes that by reminding us of these things we will not do what God has called us to do due to feelings of unworthiness. Satan wants us to believe that our prayers and our efforts to please God are futile. If I listened to all of the things that Satan told me about myself, I would have stopped preaching years ago. What prevents me from

Chapter 11: How To Cope With Opposition

stopping is the fact that I already know I'm not perfect and that all I'm required to do is try my best to please God by doing what I can and trusting Him to do what I can't. We all make mistakes, but we are able to recover from them through the grace of God. When Satan reminds us of our pasts, we should remind him of his future!

We must prepare ourselves early for opposition. We know that we will face it the moment we step out on faith and in obedience to God, so we should already have a plan for dealing it. When Nehemiah was preparing to go back to Jerusalem to rebuild the wall, he acquired letters from the king which granted him permission. He knew that he would have to travel through territories filled with people who were in opposition of rebuilding the walls of the City of Jerusalem. But with those letters in his hands, he was protected. Had he gone unprepared and not anticipated the possible opposition awaiting him up ahead, it would have taken him longer to complete the project ... if he completed it at all.

HOW OPPOSITION WINS
1. Not preparing for it

Many of us do not overcome opposition because we do not make preparations for it. We have not equipped ourselves to handle opposition; and as a result, when opposition confronts us, we are defeated, and we never accomplish our tasks. Some people who go into business are not prepared for opposition. They do not anticipate unexpected repairs, periods when customers won't purchase at the anticipated rate, delays in deliveries, etc. If business owners have not prepared for these possibilities, such occurrences may just cause them to go out of business.

I encourage people, especially young people, to be prepared for any and everything because you never know what type of opposition you may face in life. You should always be prepared to stand alone. Take advantage of the opportunity to go to school or learn a trade. When you have knowledge and a skill set, no one can take that away from you; and if something unexpected occurs and things do not happen the way you plan for them to, you will always have something to fall back on. Being prepared with knowledge and skills is necessary for all age groups. Modern technology is constantly improving and information becomes obsolete at an amazingly fast pace. Everyone needs to keep abreast of the changes so that we can be prepared.

2. Not expecting it

Opposition should not be surprising to us—it is natural. Let us use the animal kingdom as our example. Every animal faces opposition because there is another animal who regards it as prey or wants what it has. It is a part of each animal's daily activity to seek after its prey. This is the same concept that is at work between the devil and Christians: we are his prey. The Bible tells us, "Your adversary the devil, as a roaring lion, walketh about, seeking whom he may devour" (I Peter 5:8). The devil sends opposition our way because he does not want us to trust God.

Satan did not want the walls of Jerusalem to be rebuilt, but because Nehemiah was prepared and the people

Chapter 11: How To Cope With Opposition

were willing to work, the walls were rebuilt. Satan did not give up, though. But realizing that there would be more opposition to face, Nehemiah went to God in prayer. Notice that he went to God ahead of time. He did not wait until the opposition was upon him. He had already anticipated it.

While the walls were being built, the enemies of Jerusalem were enraged "and conspired all of them together to come and to fight against Jerusalem, and to hinder it" (Nehemiah 4:8). The next step of the devil's plan of opposition was to have the walls torn down by the enemies. When Nehemiah heard of this plan, he prayed and "set a watch against them day and night" (Nehemiah 4:9). He prepared himself and his men for opposition. "Every one with one of his hands wrought in the work, and with the other hand held a weapon" (Nehemiah 4:17).

3. Not praying and discerning

Some of us do not overcome opposition because we do not pray, watch, and work. Some of us want to watch without praying, and others want to pray without watching; still, others want to watch and work without praying, and others want to pray without watching and working. It is important that we do all three of these. We should not stop praying while we are working on an assignment. Prayer gives us continued strength to complete the task. If we rely on prayer alone, no work will be done. No project can be completed without work. So, never stop working, but watch while you work. Be armed with the weapons of your warfare!

4. Allowing it to distract us from our goal(s)

Satan uses opposition to distract us. He wants to divert our attention away from the things of God. When we lose focus on God, our goals and assignments will never be completed. We will be focusing on everything except the things we should be focusing on. When you are working on a wall for God, then your focus should be the wall. You should watch the people passing by, but do not become distracted by them and then stop working.

STAY FOCUSED

Nehemiah faced opposition continuously while he rebuilt the walls of Jerusalem. Every time he was opposed, he was able to defeat those who came against him. Eventually, the walls were finished. When his enemies saw that he had completed the assignment God had given him, "they were much cast down in their own eyes: for they perceived that this work was wrought of our God" (Nehemiah 6:16).

When you are in the will of God and are working on the task(s) He has assigned to you, He will bless you in the midst of your opposition. Your wall can be built if you pray, watch, and work consistently. When your wall is complete, despite the opposition, it will be evident that the Lord was with you, and the wall will stand as a testament to God's power over the enemy!

CHAPTER 12: HOW TO COPE WITH REJECTION

"Now the Lord of peace himself gives you peace always by all means. The Lord be with you all." (11 Thessalonians 3:16)

REJECTION MEANS "THE REFUSAL TO ACCEPT, SUBMIT to, believe, or make use of something; to refuse to consider or deny; to refuse to recognize or give affection to." Rejection is a common occurrence that takes many forms. In general, people like to be accepted, but they have a difficult time dealing with rejection. Rejection causes different reactions in different people. We will discuss these reactions and how they should be handled.

WRONG WAYS OF DEALING WITH REJECTION
1. Become rebellious

A common reaction to rejection is rebelliousness. People who have been rejected have a tendency to resist others, mainly because they are angry about having been rejected. When people rebel, they choose to be uncooperative and disagree with anything that is said or done—this is not because they do not understand or believe what is being said or done, but because they do not want to be a part of anything; they become difficult to work with, and people do not enjoy their company. Rebelliousness is a defense mechanism used to protect people from the pain of rejection.

2. Feeling inferior
Another reaction is inferiority. When people are rejected, they begin to feel that they do not meet the standards of others; they develop a poor self-image. As a result of this, they try to change things about themselves in an effort to be accepted. Normally, they are not comfortable with the changes they make because they do not represent their true being.

3. Running from your problems and feelings
Escapism is also a reaction to rejection. People who are rejected often try not to deal with the realities of their situations; they ignore them instead, hoping that they will just go away. They will use drugs, alcohol, television, jobs, and other devices as a means of escape.

4. Developing a spirit of fear
When people are rejected, they develop a sense of fear.

Chapter 12: How To Cope With Rejection

They are afraid of everything that reminds them of the rejection. Many women are afraid of relationships with men because they have been rejected in a previous relationship. They, in turn, reject men who approach them to protect themselves from the possibility of being hurt again. Men face the same fear—if they have been hurt by a woman in a relationship, they become afraid to establish relationships with other women. We must understand that because we have experienced rejection in one relationship, that does not mean that we will experience it in another.

HOW TO DEAL WITH REJECTION

We should deal with rejection the same way Jesus did—yes, even Jesus was rejected. He was rejected by both strangers, friends, and family members. Jesus had brothers and sisters who did not believe that He was the Son of God. Even the people whom He came to save rejected Him. Jesus did not allow rejection to hinder Him from completing His assignment. Despite the reactions of others, He continued to do all of the things that He had purposed to do.

We wonder why we are rejected by friends, loved ones, and co-workers for no apparent reason. Some people who we know personally do not receive us because they know too much about us. "For Jesus himself testified, that a prophet hath no honor in his own country" (John 4:44). Some people think that by acknowledging you, they're discrediting themselves. People close to us do not receive us because they know us, whereas people who are not close to us receive us because they do not know us personally. That is just the way people are ... including you and I. It takes the wisdom of God and understanding of His Word to see people in the right light, including those you've grown up with. When we truly get into God's Word, we will learn how to stop "evaluating others from a human point of view" (2 Corinthians 5:16), and start viewing people through a spiritual lens. We will stop seeing people where they are and start seeing where God is taking them, and also stop judging them for the current problems and start envisioning them in their future glorious state. Most importantly, we will receive the wisdom to respect authority, no matter who holds that authority (1 Peter 5, Luke 16).

Because we mainly focus on the disappointed that we feel as a result of being rejected, we often overlook the fact that rejection occurs in the lives of Christians for specific purposes. Sometimes we are rejected because God does not want us to glory in our accomplishments. Many times, when people succeed, we'll boast "I did it!" The very thing(s) that we are boastful of often becomes the very same things that causes others to reject us. You boast about establishing your own business, but out of jealousy those who you expect to support you refuse to patronize your business. You boast about the things you have done for others while forgetting about the things God has done for you which put you in a position to do for others; but when those you help refuse to acknowledge you or even show appreciation for what you did, you feel rejected. The truth is, whenever we take the credit for what God has done for us and through us, we set ourselves up to be rejected.

There was once a frog who wanted to go across the lake. He was too tired to swim, so he asked a bird to help

Chapter 12: How To Cope With Rejection

him. He came up with a plan: he would hold a stick in his mouth, and the bird would hold the other end of the stick; that way, the frog would be flying with the bird as it soared through the air. The bird agreed. As they were flying, a farmer looked up and said, "What a great idea!" The frog yelled, "It was my idea." But when the frog opened his mouth to boast, he inadvertently let go of the stick and fell to the ground. When the frog landed, the farmer said, "If you had never opened your mouth to tell me it was your idea, you would be on the other side by now!" Do not let your desire to be recognized, acknowledged, and praised by others keep you from reaching your destination.

God will allow us to be rejected in order to move us in another place. He used this technique with Joseph. Joseph was thrown into a pit, taken to another land, sold by strangers, accursed of rape, imprisoned, and forgotten before he was made ruler over Egypt. Before all of this took place, God had shown Joseph in a dream that he would be ruler over his brothers. It was because of this dream that all of his troubles began. The final manifestation of the dream did not occur until Joseph had experienced a number of rejections (Genesis 37, 39-41).

We may not understand rejection while it is taking place, but if we take the time to look back, we'll see God's hand at work. Every rejection that we ever encountered has served to move us forward into the things that God has planned for us. In order for us to receive certain things, we have to be denied other things through rejection. Sometimes, rejection takes place in relationships. We would never meet our divinely chosen mates if we were not rejected by the mates we had chosen on our own. We would never receive new jobs if we were not rejected on previous jobs. We do not understand rejection when we are experiencing it, but it is used to teach us that we cannot depend on people because people are imperfect; they will change. We can only depend on God, "for he is the living God, and steadfast forever" (Daniel 6:26).

When God begins to show us dreams and visions of the places He plans to take us, we have to be willing to accept the rejection that will move us to those places. That is a part of the test. Do not be discouraged. However, if we have God's Word, we will be able to walk away from each rejection with a smile, knowing that we are just one step closer to our destinations. When we were preparing to build our new church, we were rejected by several banks. However, I continued to move forward because God had shown me the edifice that He desired for us to worship Him in. It was frustrating at times, but I never gave up. After being rejected by several sources, we were able to acquire financing for the project. If God shows you where He intends to take you, the day will certainly come when you will stand in that place!

Sometimes we try to enter the places God has called us to before the appropriate time. Before Moses received God's strategy to deliver the children of Israel out of their bondage in Egypt, he attempted to settle a dispute between two Hebrews. One of the men asked Moses. "Who made thee prince and a judge over us?" (Exodus 2:14). There was a set time when Moses would be the judge of the people, but he stepped out before God had instructed him to do

Chapter 12: How To Cope With Rejection

so and got rejected. God had not yet prepared Moses for his calling. We must wait on God. If we step out ahead of God's timing, we will get rejected.

We can only move into the places God has called us to when He has given us all of the keys to unlock the doors. Each time we experience rejection, we are given a new key. In order to walk in the fullness of what God has called us to, we need the keys to every door in that place. The more God has in store for us, the more keys we will need and the more rejection we will face. We will never become sorrowful due to rejection when we understand this principle, knowing that the keys that God gives to us will open doors that no man can close!

Coping with the Uncopable

CHAPTER 13: HOW TO COPE WITH STRESS

"And the apostles gathered themselves together unto Jesus, and told him all things, both what they had done, and what they had taught. And he said unto them, Come ye yourselves apart into a desert place, and rest a while: for there were many coming and going, and they had no leisure so as to eat." (Mark 6:30-32).

"Come unto me, all ye hat labor and are heavy laden, and I give you rest." (Matthew 11:28)

STRESS IS CALLED *THE SILENT KILLER*. IT IS ONE OF THE leading causes of death. Stress can cause us to suffer from numerous physical illnesses such as stomach ulcers, high blood pressure, diseases, and even total body failure. Stress is an internal reaction to external situations. People become stressed when they lose their jobs; some are stressed because of the death of a loved one; others are stressed because of the enormous responsibilities that they have. Many people today are stressed out because they are trying to exceed their limitations and do things they were never commanded or expected by God to do. Whatever the cause of our stress, we must learn how to handle it so that it does not affect us physically.

We have to know what God has called us to do and be satisfied with what He has chosen for us. Knowing our personal limitations can decrease the amount of stress we experience. Some people are stressed because they try to do everything, even things that God did not intend for them to do. He has only equipped us to do those things that He desires for us to do. When we go outside of God's will, we will not succeed, and we cause ourselves unnecessary stress.

CAUSES OF STRESS

1. High expectations

When we expect too much from other people and they do not live up to our expectations, we tend to become stressed over their failures. We must realize that people will not say and do and be everything that we'd like them to; they are individuals with their own needs and goals. We should not expect others to meet all of our expectations, especially when we consider the fact that we do not always meet the expectations of others ... including God.

Many people expect others to secure accomplish-

Chapter 13: How To Cope With Stress

ments that they are not able to secure. For instance, many Christians expect their leaders to be flawless. When they become aware of anything that does not fit into the unrealistic expectations that they have developed, they become stressed. This is unfair to both them and their leaders. We have to accept the fact that no one is perfect, "For all have sinned and come short of the glory of God" (Romans 3:23). If we do not realize that everyone makes mistakes, we will always get stressed when people do not meet our expectations and exemplify perfection.

2. A lack of rest
Jesus taught the disciples how to handle stress. They had been going across the countryside teaching men and women about Jesus, and they were enjoying the work that they we doing for the Lord. When they came to report to Jesus all that had taken place, they were excited. Jesus, recognized that they were stressed but did not realize it because of their excitement, instructed them to rest.

Rest is important. We have physical bodies, which have limitations. It is necessary for us too make sure that our bodies get the appropriate rest. Even Jesus had to rest. Although He was God, He was still in the flesh; and while on earth, His flesh required that He eat, sleep, and rest just like the rest of us.

Jesus did not tell His disciples to rest where they were; instead, He told them to pull away and find someplace quiet. We cannot rest properly when there is a lot of activity going on around us. We must find a quiet place. When we are seeking rest, we should limit the amount of noise around us—we can do this by separating ourselves from the crowds. Sometimes we need to turn off the television and the radio and have total silence. When there is silence, we can hear God speaking to us.

A MEDICINE CALLED LAUGHTER

Once we receive the rest that we need and take the time to hear from God, the next thing we need to do is get together with family and friends for fun and laughter. Laughter helps us deal with stress. When we laugh, we release much of the stress we carry off of us. There are many things that can make us laugh: we can watch sitcoms and comedies that are parodies of every day life, and we can play games that are fun and challenging and make us laugh. We should never become so serious that we do not take time to laugh. Psalms 17:22 declares, "A merry heart doeth good like a medicine."

Since we know causes of stress and its effects, it is our duty not to allow stress to overtake our bodies and lives. The Apostle Paul instructed us to present our bodies as living sacrifices, holy, acceptable unto God (Romans 12:1). If we don't take care of our bodies by monitoring our stress levels and properly disposing of stress, we jeopardize what God can do in and through us. We need to overcome our stress because stress is not an acceptable practice to God. It has a negative impact on our physical bodies and our emotional well-being. No, God is not pleased when we allow stress to overtake us. He wants us to be healthy, and to do so, we must bring the things that stress us to Him so that He may give us rest and peace of mind!

CHAPTER 14: HOW TO COPE WITH WORRY

"Therefore I say unto you, Take no thought for your life, what ye shall eat or what ye shall drink; nor yet for your body, what ye shall put on. Is not the life more than meat, and the body more than raiment? Behold the fowls of the air: for they sow not, neither do they reap, nor gather into barns; yet your heavenly Father feedeth them. Are ye not much better than they?" (Matthew 6:25-26)

EVERYONE WORRIES ABOUT SOMETHING AT SOME point in time. Some people think that Christians don't worry, but they do. Worrying is simply a way of life for most people; they have worried about things for so long they don't know any other way to live, they don't know how to relax. Worrying can become a habit, especially considering that it is one of the easiest things to do. No one has to work hard to worry, nor do they have to pay a fee. Worry makes itself available to anyone who is interested in doing it.

People worry *when* things do not turn out the way they want them to. People worry *that* things won't turn out the way they want them to. We usually pray for God to show up and perform an instant miracle on our behalves because we do not want to tarry and wait for anything. If it were left up to us, we would choose not go to the doctor and have tests run on us, nor take medication; we would prefer, instead, that God simply heal us instantly. We do not want to go through situations that teach us patience; instead, we want God to do things for us instantly; we want Him to deliver us from our habits instantly. God is able to perform instant miracles, but He does not always choose to do so. Many times, God will walk us through our trials and tests instead of preventing us from experiencing them; He'll walk with us through the Valley of the Shadow of Death, not lead us around the valley. There is a lesson to be learned in every experience that we encounter.

SIGNS OF A PERSON WHO LOVES TO WORRY
1. They feel worthless and powerless

When people worry, they feel worthless; they do not feel as if they possess enough, can give enough, or can do enough; they have forgotten what they are really worth. Jesus uses birds to show us that we are worth more than we think. He tells us that, though the birds do not sow, reap, or gather food, God still feeds them. Jesus then asked us, "Are ye

Chapter 14: How To Cope With Worry

not much better than they?" (Matthew 6:26). The point He was making is this: if God will do all of these things for the birds, then He will do much more for you and I. This does not mean that blessings are going to just fall into our laps. The Lord provides food for the birds, but they must go out and get it their food. As the old saying goes: The early bird always get the worm. Get up and pursue after the blessing. Don't just sit there.

2. They only talk about their problems

People who love to worry love to tell others about their troubles. Worrying does not only affect the person worrying, but it affects those around them. The people they talk to about their troubles usually begin to develop compassion for them, and consequently, they begin to become worried also. Worried people love to transfer their fear and anxiety to others. When husbands worry, their wives worry. When wives worry, their husbands worry. When parents worry, their children worry. When children worry, their parents worry. When one friend worries, the other friend begins to worry. When people care about us, they tend to worry when we get worried. If this continues to happen, everyone will end up worrying rather than seeking God for direction. Focus on the solutions, not the problems.

3. They focus on things they can't change or control

Sometimes we worry about things that are of no concern to us. The question we should ask ourselves is whether or not what we are worrying about is worth worrying about.

Most of the time our answer will be "No"—worrying is not worth it because there is nothing that we can do about certain situations. Worry is not going to change the situation, nor make it disappear; it only adds to the difficulty of the problem. Extensive worrying can lead to depression.

THE SIN OF WORRY

God is disappointed when we worry. He does not like to see us sitting with our heads down, wondering how we will eat or clothe ourselves and our families. He does not want us worrying about what the doctors will say about our health, or what the creditors will say about our finances, or the judges will say about our cases. God wants us to put all of our cares in His hands. He wants to show us that He is our Doctor, Lawyer, and our Provider. It is not our job to take care of ourselves; it is His.

We must learn to cooperate with God and do what He instructs us to do. We may not understand what He is telling us to do sometimes, but His instructions are the solution to our worries; they are His prescription for our anxiety. When God tells us to love our enemies, we have to shake it and take it. When He tells us to smile at those who are frowning, we have to shake it and take it. Do not question God about the medicine that He prescribes for you because He is The Great Physician. He knows what your sickness is and He knows exactly what it takes to cure you.

HOW TO DEFEAT WORRY

When we find ourselves worrying about things which we

Chapter 14: How To Cope With Worry

have no control over, we need to stand on the promises of God. God's promises are found throughout the Bible, and they remind us of the things God is able to do. We are not alone. Our Father in heaven loves us. Listed below are several scriptures that contain the promises of God. Use them when you find yourself being overtaken by worry:

--Thou wilt keep him in perfect peace, whose mind is stayed on thee; because he trusteth in thee. Trust ye in the Lord forever: for in the Lord JEHOVAH IS EVERLASTING STRENGTH (Isaiah 26: 3-4).

> "Fret not thyself because of evildoers, neither be thou envious against the workers of iniquity. For they shall soon be cut down like the grass, and wither as the green herb. Trust in the Lord, and do good; so shalt thou dwell in the land, and verily thou shalt be fed." (Psalms 37:1-3)

> "I have been young, and now am old; yet have I not seen the righteous forsaken, nor his seed begging bread." (Psalms 37:25)

> "For the Lord God is a sun and shield: the Lord will give grace and glory: no good thing will He withhold from them that walk uprightly." (Psalms 84:11)

> He will show me the path of life: in thy presence is fullness of joy; and thy right hand there are plea-

sures for evermore." (Psalms 16:11)

These are but a few reminders of God's goodness to us as Christians. Rest assured that there is a promise for everything that you may experience in this life.

I have shared with you key steps on how to reclaim your joy by managing your emotions when in tough situations. These are things I had to learn how to do, the great men and women of faith in the Bible had to learn how to do, and other individuals throughout history had to learn how to do. Everyone is emotional—we were designed to be like our Creator who is an emotional being. But God also knows how to manage His emotions, and He urges us to practice mastery over ours. Don't be ruled by how you feel; instead, learn how to take back the power over your life by regulating your emotions and bringing them under subjection to God's Word. Through Christ and the Holy Spirit, you are able to do "all things" (Philippians 4:13).

Pick up the Sermon Series
"Coping with the Uncopable"
by Rev. Timothy Flemming, Sr.

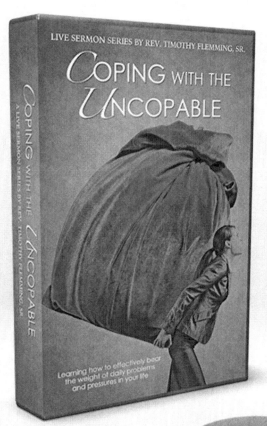

14 messages that will teach you how to effectively manage your emotions

Available on CD and DVD

Order at www.MCBCATL.org or call (404) 344-0343

ABOUT THE AUTHOR

Reverend Timothy Flemming, Sr. was born December 31, 1950 in Macon, GA. He is a community leader and activist. As a youth, Rev. Flemming preached his first sermon at the age of 11 at the Ross Street Baptist Church in Pinehurst, GA. He has since pastured five churches around the state of Georgia. Rev. Flemming, Sr. received a diploma in Theology from the American Baptist Theological Extension Seminary in Nashville, TN. He studied two years at Mercer University in Macon, GA. and earned a BA in 1986 from Morehouse College in Atlanta, GA. After his studies at the National Theological Seminary and College of Baltimore Maryland, he was awarded a Masters of Divinity degree and a Doctorate of Ministry degree.

As a community activist, he, along with Rev. P. Henderson Little, in 1967, led a protest in Macon, GA. against the city's discriminatory practice of not hiring African American policemen and denying African American graduates employment opportunities. Rev. Flemming also founded the Greenbriar Merchant Business Association and hosts the Southwest Community Restoration Association. In 1988, Rev. Flemming joined former President of the Southern Christian Leadership Conference (SCLC), Rev. Joseph E. Lowery, in a protest against those banks in Atlanta that were discriminating against small African American businesses and churches. Also, in 2006, he was sworn in as a local board member of the SCLC and was awarded the Living Legend Award at Georgia State University. In 1983, Rev. Flemming was the first African American preacher to host "Moments of Reflection" on CBS affiliate Channel 5 in Atlanta, GA. In 1985, he received the H.J. Ross Research Award as one of the sixteen outstanding personality of the south. In 1986, Rev. Flemming was the recipient of the prestigious Gospel Music Workshop of America, Inc. (GMWA) and Stellar Award for spoken word for the sermon "What Jealousy Will Do". The late Edmond Patterson, radio announcer for WAOK, awarded Rev. Flemming with the "Preacher of the Year" award at the Atlanta Civic Center with over 10,000 in attendance. Upscale Magazine has twice listed him as one of America's greatest preachers. Because of his singing talent, he has also been given the nickname "The Little Man with the Big Voice". He has had the opportunity to preach and sing around the world in such faraway countries as Mexico, Israel, the Bahamas, Germany, France, Trinidad, and Singapore. He was also the first African American preacher to minister in Calcutta, India. In 1985, while in Switzerland, he was also rewarded with the title "Mr. Versatility" in sacred music. In January of 1996, Dr. Henry J. Lyons, former President of the National Baptist Convention, appointed him to be the Director of Media Ministry of the National Baptist Convention. Rev. Flemming was later appointed to the National Council of Churches in America to be the National Baptist Convention's voice. He was awarded the Martin Luther King, Jr. award and honored by Rev. Hosea Williams with the Martin Luther King Medallion for his unyielding leadership in serving the homeless. In 1998, Rev. Flemming was awarded with the Mahalia Jackson/Thomas Dorsey Award as one of America's greatest male gospel singers. Also, that same year he preached the world famous sermon "Snakes in the Church" before an audience of over 50,000 Baptists as well as then President of the United States of America, Bill Clinton, in Orlando, FL. The New York Times wrote that Rev. Flemming "proved to be the sonorous, Bible-fulminating orator and gifted firebrand pulpiteer of our times" (September 7, 1996).

Recognized for his keen insight, Rev. Flemming served on the Advisory Board of former Atlanta mayor, Bill Campbell, in 1995. In 1997, Rev. Flemming was inducted into the Georgia Hall of Fame as an outstanding citizen of the state of Georgia. He has been invited on numerous occasions to the White House to serve on the Clergy Advisory Committee under the leadership of former Presidents Jimmy Carter, Bill Clinton, and former Vice President Al Gore.

Rev. Flemming is the pastor of the Mount Carmel Baptist Church with a membership of over ten thousand members in two locations—in Southwest Atlanta and Midtown Atlanta. Millions across the nation are captivated by Rev. Flemming's broadcast which airs weekly on the Word Network and Channel 57 WATC. After the tragedy of 911 in New York City, Rev. Flemming's "It is a mean old world to live in" taken from his Old Time Camp Meeting Songs was aired as a public service announcement on CNN and heard around the world. It proved so successful that CNN later contacted him again to do another public service announcement, this time using another one of his Old Time Camp Meeting Songs "I can't hardly get along in this world".

As a man of business man, he is founder and CEO of God's Strength Records, a gospel recording label which features artists such as Margaret Davie-Maddox, Katie Graham of Jackson, MS; the Mount Carmel Mass Choir; and the young, energetic and dynamic Praise Breakers of Mount Carmel. As a legendary praise song vocalist, Rev. Flemming has released over 10 highly praised gospel albums including Got the Devil Under My Feet and He's A High Class Physician. He is also the author of "Coping with the Uncopable", a book which deals with the fundamental building blocks of the emotions.

Rev. Flemming is the husband of Mrs. Virginia Lee Jackson-Flemming (for over 40 years), the father of three sons, and grandfather of four.